LISTEN WISE

LISTEN WISE

Teach Students to Be
Better Listeners

Monica Brady-Myerov

JB JOSSEY-BASS™
A Wiley Brand

Copyright © 2021 by John Wiley & Sons, Inc. All rights reserved.

Jossey-Bass
A Wiley Imprint
111 River St, Hoboken, NJ 07030
www.josseybass.com

No part of this publication may be reproduced, stored in a retrieval system, or transmitted in any form or by any means, electronic, mechanical, photocopying, recording, scanning, or otherwise, except as permitted under Section 107 or 108 of the 1976 United States Copyright Act, without either the prior written permission of the Publisher, or authorization through payment of the appropriate per-copy fee to the Copyright Clearance Center, Inc., 222 Rosewood Drive, Danvers, MA 01923, phone +1 978 750 8400, fax +1 978 750 4470, or on the web at www. copyright.com. Requests to the Publisher for permission should be addressed to the Permissions Department, John Wiley & Sons, Inc., 111 River Street, Hoboken, NJ 07030, phone + 1 201 748 6011, fax +1 201 748 6008, or online at www.wiley. com/go/permissions.

Limit of Liability/Disclaimer of Warranty: Although the publisher and author have used their best efforts in preparing this book, they make no representations or warranties with respect to the accuracy or completeness of the contents of this book and specifically disclaim any implied warranties of merchantability or fitness for a particular purpose. No warranty may be created or extended by sales representatives or written sales materials. The advice and strategies contained herein may not be suitable for your situation. You should consult with a professional where appropriate. Neither the publisher nor author shall be liable for any loss of profit or any other commercial damages, including but not limited to special, incidental, consequential, or other damages.

Jossey-Bass books and products are available through most bookstores. To contact Jossey-Bass directly, call our Customer Care Department within the U.S. at 800-956-7739, outside the U.S. at +1 317 572 3986, or fax +1 317 572 4002.

Wiley also publishes its books in a variety of electronic formats and by print-on-demand. Some material included with standard print versions of this book may not be included in e-books or in print-on-demand. If this book refers to media such as a CD or DVD that is not included in the version you purchased, you may download this material at http://booksupport.wiley.com. For more information about Wiley products, visit www.wiley.com.

Library of Congress Cataloging-in-Publication Data is Available:

ISBN 9781119755494 (hardback)
ISBN 9781119755531 (ePDF)
ISBN 9781119755524 (ePUB)

Cover design: Wiley
Cover image: © Brandon Laufenberg/Getty Images

FIRST EDITION

SKY10025529_030821

Contents

Acknowledgments

I would never have started Listenwise and thus had the experience to write this book if my husband Adam Brady-Myerov hadn't listened to me when I said I had an idea. He didn't poke holes in it or ask whether I was qualified to be an edtech entrepreneur, he just listened and said "Go for it." I want to thank him for always listening. And to my children, who have taught me so much, thank you for your love, support, and patience.

I want to thank many people for helping me with this book. Thank you to my sister Liz Witherspoon for editing as I wrote and being so supportive. Thanks to Aja Frost, a former intern and friend, for helping me first get the ideas on paper. I want to thank Alistair Van Moere, the Director of Product for MetaMetrics, for co-writing the chapter on assessing listening. Also thanks to Heather Koons of MetaMetrics for her contributions to the listening and reading chapter. Christin Wheeler, a reading specialist, shared valuable insights with me. Rachel Kramer Theodorou, a professor at Brandeis University, contributed her expertise with English learners. My team at Listenwise has been a huge help and inspiration. I could never have done this without Karen Gage, my business partner and friend. Dr. Marielle Palombo, Director of Curriculum, provided valuable insights and many, many edits to the book. Without team members Adam Buchbinder, Chelsea Murphy, Erica Petersen, Matt Pini, and Vicki Krupp I never would have learned so much about listening as we grew the company together. Thank you to the many teachers who have provided their insights and stories for this book, especially Jim Bentley and Scott Petri.

Thank you to my mother for telling me I could do anything I wanted and pushing me to do it. And to my father for asking me to read him the *New York Times* while he drove. Reading out loud to my father launched me on this path and I dedicate this book to his memory.

Introduction

My students don't listen!

That's what almost every teacher says when I tell them that, after a career as an NPR reporter, I have started an education company focused on listening. They tell me they must repeat themselves when explaining how the Civil War got started. Or demonstrate a math concept over and over. They give simple homework directions in multiple ways. They call out to students many times before they have their attention. They lament that their students are poor listeners.

Might every student struggle with this most basic skill? Listening. If you were to stop a hundred teachers at an education conference and ask them this question, as I have, you will find that yes, listening is something that teachers report most students don't know how to do well. And teachers are at a loss for what to do about it. This book will help.

Listening is a skill that can be modeled, taught, and improved. I have learned this on my journey from an award-winning public radio reporter to the founder of an education technology start-up called Listenwise, a website for K–12 teachers that uses the power of audio stories to advance listening and literacy skills in all students.

HOW THIS BOOK IS ORGANIZED

I organized this book to build the case for teaching listening, but also as a practical guide for K–12 teachers interested in using audio in their teaching, with class activities sprinkled throughout the book. The strategies and activities include suggestions for elementary students and middle/high school students. Readers should start from the beginning and work through to the end for the most comprehensive understanding of how and why to teach listening comprehension. However, you can also jump to the chapter on English learners or listening and reading, if that's where your interest lies. I structured the book to start with and build on academic research and my personal experience in the field as a reporter, because I've learned many people need to be convinced that listening can and should be taught because it will help their students' overall academic performance. That's why I've now devoted my career to it as the founder of Listenwise.com.

Throughout the book, I mention specific audio stories and podcasts that demonstrate a concept or could be used in a class activity. The original source of the audio is referenced in the endnotes, but you can also hear the audio and use fully developed lessons by going to https://listenwise.com/book, where you will have free access to Listenwise Premium for a period of time. Listenwise. com should be considered a digital companion to this book, so I encourage you to engage your ears as well as your eyes as you read.

In the opening chapter, "My Love of Audio Storytelling," I share my experiences as a journalist and how it shaped my love of audio. It explains how my passion turned into a desire to help students learn through listening and become better listeners.

In Chapter 2, "Listening Is a Skill," I show you that listening is a skill that can be taught, practiced, improved, and successfully demonstrated on standardized tests. It's a skill that needs to be taught because it's critical to success in college, career, and life. Curriculum standards in all 50 states include listening as a component for K–12 students. Listening skills rose to prominence with the adoption of the Common Core by many states in 2009. The standards across the states require teachers to include purposeful listening in their instruction. And, of course, listening is required in teaching students to speak English.

Chapter 3, "This Is Your Brain on Listening," looks at how listening is a complex neurological construct that involves multiple areas of the brain. Listening requires more from your brain than many other skills. You will learn from the latest neuroscientists, cognitive scientists, and communications and psychology experts. Hearing isn't all that is involved in listening, but it is a critical part. One neuroscientist explains that "sounds are among the most common and powerful stimuli for emotions."[1] Listening triggers a variety of parts of the brain to create a "movie in your mind."

You can dig into Chapter 4, "How to Teach Listening," to learn actionable techniques for teaching your students. I will share some proven strategies to improve listening. Whether you are a third-grade teacher using listening strategies to improve reading, or an 11th-grade teacher aiming to improve your students' listening skills for the workforce, this chapter gives you practical ways to start incorporating more listening into your teaching. It shows you how including listening in your instruction can teach academic vocabulary and curriculum content and help students practice reading.

You might not be a reading teacher, so you might not have considered how listening can help your students read. But Chapter 5 may change your thinking. In "The Intersection Between Listening and Reading," you learn why I believe listening is the missing piece of the literacy puzzle. Despite dozens of new approaches, techniques, and programs, the average national fourth- and eighth-grade reading scores are stagnant. There is an interdependency between listening comprehension and reading comprehension. In general, the poor reader is also likely to be a poor listener. Listening is a foundational part of teaching students how to read, yet by the middle grades it virtually disappears from our classrooms. In this chapter, you learn how using listening regularly in your classroom at any grade level can help improve reading.

Listening is a critically important skill to learning a new language. Chapter 6, "English Learners and Listening," explores how listening is critical to second language acquisition. Many of you have English language learners (ELs) in your classrooms. As the population of ELs continues to grow in our schools, every teacher needs to know how to help these learners use their listening skills to acquire knowledge and language. Listening is an important way to do that. I'll share with you some ways to differentiate instruction for ELs.

In Chapter 7, "Assessing Listening," which was co-written with Alistair Van Moere, the Chief Product Officer at MetaMetrics, we look at how even though the majority of our time is spent listening there's been very little research on how to track and improve listening as a skill. Up until recently, listening skills have been self-reported. Despite the correlation between listening and reading, there hasn't been a reliable way to break down and assess listening. This chapter reveals the new ways that listening is being measured in the classroom with the new Lexile® Framework for Listening.

Once you've learned how to improve your students' listening skills, you can learn how to help them create their own audio stories. Chapter 8, "Creating Podcasts," gives you tools to put your students in the driver's seat of the hottest trend in education, podcasting. It also shares expert tips on making podcasts with your students, which can put their listening skills to work as they create their own audio stories for a wide audience.

This book focuses on the types of listening skills needed in our classrooms. It provides concrete examples and tools for K–12 teachers. While mindful, active, interpersonal listening is an important skill to build, my experience and the focus of this book is on academic listening—in other words, listening to learn. It will give you the confidence and tools you need to use audio resources to support reading, content, and language learning.

There has never been a better time for you to focus on improving your students' listening skills. Many are concerned that technology has fractured our attention and shortened our attention spans. Students need help building their listening stamina. You might think, as do many of the teachers I've met, that listening is a lost art. No one knows how to listen anymore, they say. But I argue that listening is the most fundamental and critical skill to learning, and it's in your power to help your students become the best listeners they can be.

Reference

1. Horowitz, S.S. (2013). In the beginning was the boom. In *The universal sense: How hearing shapes the mind* (pp. 126–128). New York, NY: Bloomsbury.

Chapter 1

My Love of Audio Storytelling

We can hear before we are born, but listening can take decades to develop, practice, and perfect. It took me 20 years to become an expert listener. A professional listener. And I learned that listening is a gift we can share with others.

My passion for listening began when I got my first tape recorder for Christmas (Figure 1.1). Santa delivered my Christmas wish—a bright red Panasonic cassette tape recorder. This was the 1970s, so it was shiny and rounded on the edges. It had an easy carry handle that slid up, which told me audio was meant to be portable. It had a cheap plug-in microphone, which told me I should be listening to and recording others. And it ran on batteries so I could go anywhere I wanted to capture sound. It's really one of the only gifts I remember getting as a child. I instantly fell in love with recording sound.

My recording didn't go far beyond my family. I mostly cornered my sisters and interviewed them. I conducted a hard-hitting investigative interview with my two-year-old sister about the neighbor's dog. I thought I was a reporter. I wanted to be the *60 Minutes* leading female journalist of the time, Barbara Walters. I would also secretly place the recorder under the dining room table to capture the "adult" conversation. Even at that age, I knew listening was a way to learn something new—maybe even something adults wouldn't tell me. I only have one remaining cassette tape from this time, which I've now preserved digitally.

My love of sound and journalism started to come together a few years after I got that tape recorder for Christmas. Our family would take long drives in the summer to visit relatives in Massachusetts. It took 14 hours to drive from Kentucky to Massachusetts. Being in a car with five kids was tedious for everyone, especially my dad, who was always the driver.

My father loved news and would always play CBS news at the top of the hour on the radio. But there were very few all-news stations at that time. And there was bad reception when you were driving through the mountains of West Virginia. That means there were long stretches in between the top of the hour news bulletins and he wanted to hear more news. So he brought along his newspapers. As a daily subscriber to the *New York Times* and the *Wall Street Journal*, there was plenty of news to read. But how to hear it?

My father saw a creative solution. He told his kids that anyone who wanted to read the newspaper to him while he drove got to sit in the front seat between him and my mother. This was back when the front seat was a bench that could fit three people. Today it seems dangerous.

I saw my opportunity to escape the chaos in the back seat with my three sisters and one brother. I was the second oldest, and the only volunteer. My older sister was a bookworm and preferred reading silently to block out the noise.

I sat unbelted in between my mom and dad in the front of our station wagon and read the newspaper out loud. My dad would glance over from the road and poke his finger at the next story he wanted me to read to him. I learned how to follow a jump in a newspaper story and read with some interest and emotion. Looking back on this experience with the knowledge I now have of how hearing words and content strengthen reading and learning, I am sure these experiences had a huge impact on my learning. I know they influenced my career choice. I wanted to be an audio journalist.

But I also learned that at any age, reading to someone is a gift of sharing, love, and intimacy. Hearing another human's voice, expressing words in their own unique way makes you feel closer. You could be a kindergarten teacher sharing a picture book at circle time or a middle school teacher sharing *Harry Potter* chapter by chapter. Do not underestimate the impact of your voice on your students and their ability to listen.

WHAT AUDIO JOURNALISM TAUGHT ME ABOUT LISTENING

By the time I entered college, I knew I wanted to work in audio journalism. My love of audio was deep and abiding. Working in the news department at the Brown University college radio station was an obvious choice; it gave me the training and practice I needed to become a reporter, along with an official reason to hear and share people's stories. I considered my role as a reporter to be that of a teacher. My reports taught my listeners something about the news of the day.

My college station was a unique commercial rock station run by students. It meant the news department of 95.5 WBRU in Providence, Rhode Island did not cover college campus events. We covered local and national news including murder trials, corruption, and politics. I even had the budget to take a team of reporters to cover both the Republican and Democratic conventions in 1988.

At the heart of all the stories I covered and what I was learning about audio is that hearing people's stories is powerful.

THE INTIMACY OF AUDIO

What captivates me about audio is the intimacy of the medium. Listeners can hear emotions first-hand. Anger, joy, concern, desperation, and regret. They all sound distinct in someone's voice. You can hear someone struggling not to cry, and then their voice cracks and they break down into tears. You can hear the shock, relief, and joy of someone receiving good news they didn't expect to get. Imagine right now what these emotions sound like. Maybe you are imagining your mother telling you a dear relative passed away. Or your best friend telling you she just got engaged.

Listening to audio sharpens your ears and senses and transports you into the story. I can type "sigh," and you can imagine what it sounds like. But hearing someone mourning the loss of their loved one and saying "I am going to miss them so much" and then deeply, audibly sigh, can't be fully captured in print.

Listening to audio stories can help to engage students in stories, in literacy, and in learning. You may know this from watching kids, mouths agape, listening to you read aloud, voicing each character with expression, adding drama to your delivery to create suspense. You may not realize how much more you can do to incorporate audio into your teaching with similar effect.

Class Activity: Listening to Emotion

In the stories below, your students will be able to hear the emotion. You might spark reflective conversation after listening to the story together with some general follow-up questions: How do you think the person in the story feels? What emotions do you think that person is feeling by listening to the tone of their voice? What do pauses sometimes tell you about how a person is feeling? Do you think your voice sounds different whether you are happy or sad?

Elementary School Students: The story "50 Years After She Was Struck By Lightning, Reconnecting With The Girl Who Saved Her" is a conversation between two older women who have an emotional reunion. [1]

Middle/High School Students: The story "Trying Not To Break Down—A Homeless Teen Navigates Middle School" is full of emotion from a boy who is homeless and working hard to succeed in school and life. [2]

The story "How a Stuffed Toy Monkey Reunited a Holocaust Survivor with Relatives" is a moving conversation between a father and son about what really happened to his family during the Holocaust. [3]

The audio and additional teaching resources can be found at https://listenwise.com/book.

It's hard to get the same kind of intimate connection through just the written word. In fact, it might take a paragraph to explain in detail the emotion someone expressed in one word through their voice. And it will never capture what it sounded like to actually be there.

Previously, I studied abroad in Kenya and lived in Nairobi for the summer working as an intern for Reuters, a leading international wire service. As an intern, I mostly organized files and typed up stories from reporters calling in from the field. But one day, Mother Teresa, the Roman Catholic nun, now a saint, who worked with the poor came to Nairobi to meet with city officials to ask them to give her mission free municipal water. Reuters sent me to cover her visit to the Missionary of Charity Order in a heavily populated poor area of the city. Armed with my notebook only, because Reuters didn't have an audio service (or a podcast), I set out. Even though I didn't record Mother Teresa, I will never forget her calm, quiet, soothing voice amid the chaos of the noisy neighborhood. She was a petite woman, dressed as always in her white with blue-striped nun's habit. Physically she didn't command attention. But her sure, strong voice did.

After graduating, I returned to Nairobi, Kenya, this time as an audio journalist.

My time as a freelancer in Kenya was a launch pad into audio storytelling as I covered East Africa for Voice of America and other shortwave stations. It was during a tumultuous time in Kenya's history under a fairly new democratic government. Kenya was a British colony until it became fully independent in 1963. In 1982, the government amended the constitution, making Kenya officially a one-party state. By the time I arrived and started reporting in 1989, the government was cracking down on budding political opposition to the autocratic President Daniel arap Moi. The president had announced there would be multiparty elections but he and his government would not tolerate any criticism.

But dissent to Moi's repressive regime was rising in the poorer sections of Nairobi, especially in Kibera, the same neighborhood as Mother Teresa's mission. I knew it was my duty to hear it. I drove there with my recorder. I could hear shouting and banging nearby but didn't see anything. I was told police and rioters were clashing with opposition rioters using sticks and rocks just over the hill. I started interviewing people about their views on a multiparty democracy that didn't let the opposition make their voices heard. Suddenly a surge of people came over the hill, and surrounded my car. With my tape recorder running, I jumped back inside the car and locked the doors. The crowd was angry and violent.

I listened to the crowd get angrier around my car. And then I heard the first thud. Someone hit the car with a rock. It was time to leave. Carefully, but quickly, I drove through the crowd navigating around the people as the car was hit, pelted, and then slammed with rocks and sticks. The car was battered but I was unharmed and I had captured it all on my recorder.

What I learned is that audio requires you to be close to the action. When you are listening to audio, you are in the scene like the reporter, and that makes audio storytelling powerful. And its power can be used in your classroom.

Audio also allowed me to get very up close with gorillas. With my base in Nairobi, I covered all of East Africa reporting on events in Tanzania, Somalia, and Sudan. One of my goals was to see gorillas up close in the wild and tell their story with sound. Fueled by stories and images of Jane Goodall and her study of chimpanzees in the wild, I set off to document the sound of gorillas in what was then called Zaire, now the Democratic Republic of Congo.

I recorded our two-day trek as our guide used audio and physical clues to find the gorillas. He would see tree branches trampled in a certain way and shush our group so he could hear something inaudible to the rest of us. Silence on the hike was required. It was imperative that, when we discovered the family of silverback gorillas, we did not surprise them. The gorillas have a home area of about 12 square miles. They could have been any where as they roamed about looking for food.

With one gesture of his hand, our guide told us to stop and not move. Less than 20 feet away was a family of gorillas. I raised my mic to them, but we were too far away to capture anything more than general bird and forest sounds. So I crept closer. What struck me is how quiet the gorillas were. Aside from the occasional snort that sounded more like a pig or a horse, they silently munched on branches. I thought I would be capturing the sound of the gorillas in the natural habitat. When that sound was not distinctive, I learned an important lesson about audio journalism.

WRITING FOR LISTENING

Writing in an audio story is as critical as the sound. In the gorilla story, I used words to describe the scene, explain the silence, and enhance what audio I had. Simple, direct sentences work best in audio storytelling. Good writing for audio is active and succinct. Later, I would learn how critical this is for students to learn, too, as they develop their own writing skills. Audio journalism can teach them valuable lessons about active voice, descriptive writing, and perspective.

Now a word about video. At this point you might be thinking, what about a video clip of the gorillas or someone crying or shouting in anger? The next time you see an emotional scene on TV, mute the audio. What happens? You lose connection with the scene unfolding. Hearing stimulates emotions. Additionally, seeing a video can turn you into a bit of a lazy listener. For example, if you're shown a picture of a crying mother, you see her grief as only hers, rather than forming a mental picture of what she might look like using a composite of things familiar in your life. I explore in more detail how audio engages the mind later in the book.

When writing for audio, you can't rely on pictures to tell the story, you must use your words in the most descriptive way possible. Writing for broadcast involves using shorter, more active sentences. Newspaper or magazine writing often employs long complex sentences, but that does not work for audio. Writing for broadcast needs to take into account that you need to breathe while reading, creating natural pauses. People are usually doing another activity while listening, so I was often told to write at a fourth-grade level. At the time, I didn't know there existed reading measures such as the Lexile Framework for Reading, but I understood I needed to make my sentences short, declarative, and straightforward. Most people listen to a story, or a conversation, only once, often not giving it their full attention, and can't rewind to hear it again. It must be easy to understand the first time.

Class Activity: Writing Style—Audio versus Print

Middle/High School Students: To demonstrate the difference between writing for print and writing for audio, select a story that has been covered by the national press. If using an article on the internet, try to find one reprinted from the hard copy newspaper, not the abbreviated web version of the story. Now find the same topic covered on NPR. Select a student to read the first few paragraphs of the newspaper story out loud, then play the first minute of the NPR story, including the host introduction. Ask students to comment on the different writing style, vocabulary, and sentence structure. Discuss the facts covered in the section, but focus more on writing style than content.

Thrilled by the excitement of capturing audio and telling stories overseas, I left Kenya and moved to Rio de Janeiro, Brazil to continue working as a freelance radio journalist. Listening and recording people's stories in Portuguese was just as powerful as it was in English.

AUDIO AND LEARNING A LANGUAGE

In Brazil, I was plunged into Portuguese, which I studied in college, but really couldn't speak. Learning a new language gave me a new appreciation for listening. Listening is the first step to learning a new language. It is crucial to understanding. In a later chapter I share best practices for English learners and the impact listening skills can have on their acquisition of academic language.

What I first learned about really listening to someone else speaking a foreign language is that emotion is universally heard. I didn't need to understand every word or phrase to listen for anger, amazement, or love in someone's speech. It was conveyed in the tone of their voice, the pauses in the phrasing, and the speed of their speech. When I covered anticorruption rallies, the shouting protestors sounded frustrated, angry, and sometimes resigned. I understood emotions from watching Brazilian soap operas or "novelas."

I didn't know it at the time, but I was learning an important lesson in how listening plays a role in language acquisition while watching Brazilian soap operas. The underlying requirement for anyone to learn to speak a language is to listen to that language. By day, speaking to friends or attending a press conference, the language was hard to follow, the subjects jumped around, and I couldn't always keep track of the conversation. By night, watching the soap operas, I could absorb a new phrase or word and hear it repeated in a real conversation. Using TV and radio is an authentic way to improve second language acquisition, which I explore later in the book.

Learning another language through listening gave me a window into second language acquisition. As I continued to improve my Portuguese, I started to teach English to Brazilians. Because I lacked the training for teaching the basic grammar and structure for beginners, I taught intermediate to advanced English learners. There again, listening plays a key role. My students were adults who at one point in their lives had been more fluent English speakers but had lost their facility with the language. For them, the most important thing to do was to hear authentic English and respond. Our classes were informal gatherings in which we discussed topics or listened to the news in English. We focused on learning new vocabulary words, hearing each other's pronunciation, phrasing, and expression. Their homework was to read a novel or the news and be prepared to discuss it with each other. While this experience wasn't the same as what you are facing today with your students, where academic language is a key barrier to success for many English learners, I have an appreciation for how difficult it is to learn a new language and to teach a new language. Listening is a crucial part of both activities.

Another lesson I learned as a reporter that applied to teaching is that establishing a connection to and interest in a story makes it stick. It was sometimes hard for me to tell a good story if I didn't care about the subject. When I moved back to Boston and then Washington DC, I worked as a contract reporter for National Public Radio covering Congress and other national stories. Unlike my time as a freelance journalist, I was assigned what to cover. One story I remember was about whether American winemakers were violating the copyrights of French winemakers by calling their wines Burgundy or Bordeaux. This was not a high emotion story, and I didn't personally sit with any winemakers, either in the United States or France, to interview them to write their story. In fact, I didn't even taste any American and French wines. I used Congressional testimony, written reports, and phone interviews. In the end, the story I wrote, "Tax Bill: Wine," lacked the intimacy of audio that I craved. [4] And you could tell from the final report, which was a straightforward account of facts and counterpoints. There was an interesting way to tell this story, I just didn't find it because I wasn't interested in the story. Does this sound familiar?

You are asked to teach your students so many topics, skills, and standards that it's hard for them to feel connected or interested in all of them. But to learn something, you need to have that connection. Or you need to be interested enough to master the subject. As I found what interested me as a reporter, you, I hope, can find compelling audio that relates to what you are teaching to captivate your students. Even if you are not passionate about a topic, someone else might be.

PODCAST REVOLUTION

A podcast obsession is gripping the nation. More than half of all Americans 12 and older have listened to a podcast, and 40% of people between the ages of 12 and 24 listened to a podcast in the last month, at the time of writing.[1] There are an estimated 1,750,000 podcasts to listen to.[2] These podcasts will tell you the news of the day or how to make a perfectly fried egg. I see the explosion of podcasts as a renaissance for listening. There is now common acceptance that listening is an excellent way to understand the world or just be entertained by it. Whether listening to a podcast to learn about Ancient Greek history or how to manage their finances, millions of people are learning through listening. And young listeners are also tuning in. Capitalizing on this trend in your class will distinguish your teaching and captivate your students.

This trend shows that I'm not alone in my love of audio storytelling. We are on the forefront of an exciting time when audio can bring the world into the classroom, and students can use audio to share what they know with the world. Thousands of classrooms across grade levels, demographics, and locations are using podcasts in teaching, and some are creating their own podcasts.

> *I like to hear something that I never heard before and that is exciting!*
> —Daniel, fifth-grader in Elk Grove, CA

I've continued to see a rising number of conference sessions on how to podcast or use podcasts in the K–12 classroom. In 2019 at ISTE, the largest edtech conference, there were 23 sessions about podcasting during a three-day conference. This podcasting trend makes sense. The technology is accessible. The human voice is captivating. Hearing directly from someone who experienced an event is meaningful. Encouraging students to speak to others who have first-hand knowledge creates a deep and meaningful learning experience. Having students imitate well-written audio narratives helps them improve their writing. And most importantly, when students make podcasts, it gives them a voice. Making podcasts fosters authentic, passion-driven learning.

There has never been a better time, a more perfect moment, for me to share what I've learned about teaching listening through audio stories.

CREATING LISTENWISE

Later in my career, I moved to Boston and joined the reporting staff of WBUR. My husband and I had two daughters. The oldest was a born reader. I don't remember being a part of teaching her how to read. She seemed to have come home from school one day reading. My younger daughter struggled with reading. I didn't immediately recognize it as a reading problem until her second grade teacher recommended she work with the school's reading specialist. Her difficulties made her dislike reading. She would say she "hated reading."

But she did love listening. She would listen to books we read out loud to her, devouring the stories. She would listen to NPR on the radio every morning with me and ask me questions about the news. Her understanding of complex topics impressed me. It was because of her reading challenges that I thought she and other kids would benefit from learning more by listening. This was my lightbulb moment. I decided to leave my reporting career and start Listenwise.

Listenwise is a digital platform devoted to building listening skills using audio stories. Our mission is to inspire individuals to fulfill their potential through the power of listening. Our collection of more than 2,500 podcasts is organized into current events and standards-aligned lessons for teachers of grades 2–12. Every audio story has a read-along transcript and other scaffolding for struggling readers and English learners. The teaching resources are standards-aligned, and it's easy to assign a listening quiz or written assignment.

Much of the audio collection on Listenwise is free for teachers. And anyone can register for a free trial of Listenwise Premium, which includes scaffolding features and ready-to-go lessons.

It wasn't an easy decision to leave reporting and become an entrepreneur. I had known from a young age that I wanted to be a radio reporter, and I was enjoying my work immensely. But I felt that my love of audio went beyond the stories I could personally tell. My connections in the world of public radio and podcasting put me in a position to make a greater impact. I realized my passion for audio could be spread further if I created a bigger platform on which to share audio for educational purposes.

I also believe that fact-based, balanced reporting has a role to play in our education system. In fact, it's crucial to educate young citizens for our democracy to thrive. I thought it was a shame that every day, dozens of excellent stories about how government works, historical events, scientific discoveries, and human connections were heard once on the airwaves and then buried in the archives. But they held so much potential for educators and students—to build their knowledge and improve their listening skills.

One of the barriers that had to be overcome was sourcing stories that were short enough for use during a class period (~3–5 minutes in length), and that relate to the curriculum in grades 2–12. Anyone can search for Shakespeare on the NPR website, but you will be sorting through nearly 3,000 results. If you search for Shakespeare on Listenwise, you will find curated stories for the classroom that address, for example, the controversy over whether Shakespeare really wrote the works attributed to him and a story about the Juliet Club, which responds to letters written to Shakespeare's fictitious Juliet. And you could introduce a unit on Hamlet by listening to a story about a touring company that performed the play in 197 countries. Listenwise is dedicated to curating high-quality audio stories that are especially well suited for educational use and developing instructional supports to accompany them.

For middle and high school students, listening to a news story from a public radio reporter is engaging. Students like listening to the same stories that adults hear because they are authentic. They aren't what a team of education writers and producers thought an educational audio story should sound like. These are real stories with appeal to real audiences.

For elementary students, I turned to the excellent podcasts being created for kids to find the right educational content. On Listenwise, we focus on sourcing engaging stories that address English, social studies, and science topics. These podcasts are typically 15–30 minutes long, so our team edits them to a shorter length and focuses on key educational elements of the story.

It was through my work as a journalist that I came to understand and appreciate the importance of listening. My daughter showed me how essential listening skills are in learning to read. And my experience in building Listenwise into a thriving education technology company has taught me how good listening comprehension skills are critical to learning and how educationally valuable well-produced audio stories can be.

REFLECTION AND PLANNING

Take this opportunity to write some reflections and plans for action.

What are some ways you can incorporate reading aloud to your students to build a personal connection with them through audio?

_____

_____

Have you learned to speak another language as an adult? How has that experience informed your understanding of the importance of listening in language acquisition, and how can you share that experience with your students?

_____

_____

How might you find and share one audio story that you think will be interesting to your students?

_____

_____

Audio Resources

[1] Garcia-Navarro, Lulu, et al. (2018, February 4). 50 years after she was struck by lightning, reconnecting with the girl who saved her. NPR, www.npr.org/2018/02/04/582904413/50-years-after-she-was-struck-by-lightning-reconnecting-with-the-girl-who-saved-her.

[2] Peacher, Amanda. (2018, October 9). Trying not to break down—A homeless teen navigates middle school. NPR, www.npr.org/2018/10/09/653386388/trying-not-to-break-down-a-homeless-teen-navigates-middle-school.

[3] Martin, Michel. (2018, December 2). How a stuffed toy monkey reunited a Holocaust survivor with relatives. NPR, www.npr.org/2018/12/02/672758708/how-a-stuffed-toy-monkey-reunited-a-holocaust-survivor-with-relatives.

[4] Brady, Monica. (1997, July 21). Tax bill: Wine. NPR, www.npr.org/1997/07/21/1039020/tax-bill-wine.

References

1. Edison Research. (2019, March 6). "The infinite dial 2019." https://www.edisonresearch.com/infinite-dial-2019/ (accessed September 10, 2020).

2. PodcastHosting.org. (2021, January 1). "2021 global podcast statistics, demographics & habits." https://podcasthosting.org/podcast-statistics/ (accessed February 1, 2020).

Chapter 2

Listening Is a Skill

Vicki Beck's papers are spread out across her kitchen table. She can't find the one graphic organizer that she wants to use in tomorrow's science lesson. She knows she saw it on her desk in her classroom when she pulled her papers together and shoved them in her bag to take home for the weekend.

But now it's Sunday night. It's 6 o'clock. And she can't find the one paper she needs right now to pull together the lesson she's planning to teach on tadpoles and metamorphosis.

It's not until her son shouts her name for the fourth time, standing right next to her, that she hears him.

"Mom, what's for dinner?" he's practically screaming.

She is not listening. Vicki suddenly realizes she is guilty of not listening: the same behavior for which she gets so angry with her students.

"How can I teach my students to be better listeners, when I don't think I'm a good listener?" she wonders.

She thinks about how she can model better listening skills, not just in school but at home as well. She knows it's important to listen to her son, but she's not always good at it.

She stacks her papers, closes her computer, and asks her son, "How does pasta sound?"

WHY LISTENING MATTERS

There are some skills that will make you successful no matter who you are or what you're doing. The ability to listen well is unequivocally one of them. Being a good listener means you are attuned to the world. You are present and engaged. You are listening to family, friends, and coworkers and hearing and responding to what they say, the first time they say it. It means you are listening to the radio, podcasts, music, or audio books and learning from them.

Listening is often not considered a traditional skill, such as reading or multiplying. In education we are focusing more than ever on developing students' noncognitive skills such as critical thinking, problem solving, and self-control. Listening is a key social skill that needs attention. Listening is an equalizing force.

Maybe you haven't stopped to think about this essential skill. You haven't wondered if you are a good or bad listener, but trust me, others have evaluated you. And your listening ability could be holding you back or helping you to excel. Good listening skills help you learn to read, become a better learner, be more empathetic, and succeed at work and in personal relationships. Listening is the primary way we learn. It's the way we show others that we care. It's how we absorb critical information at work. It's the first and probably the last thing you will do in your life. Listen.

It is especially key to learning because effective listeners are better learners.[1] As a teacher, you can play an important role in developing your students' listening skills, just as you do when teaching them math or science. If you want to prepare your students to succeed in future jobs and careers you should think about including listening instruction in your curriculum.

And not just practicing listening skills, but tracking progress and even testing listening.

> *One of the things we hear a lot is that kids don't listen. They don't know how to pay attention. A lot of the new media is very distracting. It contributes to the flickering mind. That's why we focus on purposeful listening.*
> —Robert DeLossa, high school Social Studies department chair, Lowell, MA

And yet listening as a skill is not widely taught in K–12 curriculum in the United States, even though it is linked to both literacy and academic success.[2] When I ask teachers at all grade levels how they are teaching listening, most say they aren't explicitly teaching listening, and they wouldn't know where to begin. Some elementary teachers do teach listening. Typically, it's part of their expectations for social and emotional learning. But the focus is often on listening to others and listening to instructions. Some teachers in the lower grades have listening stations or have students listen to audio books.

More often now, upper elementary teachers and beyond ask students to both produce and listen to recordings in the form of podcasts or videos recorded by teachers, gathered from YouTube, or generated via interactive platforms like Flipgrid, but more often than not the focus is on understanding the content of what is shared and not on the act of listening itself. Some teachers who value peer feedback or reflection will coach or guide students on how to provide peer feedback that's carefully constructed to be "kind, specific, and helpful" as Ron Berger from EL Education would say, yet at the same time those teachers may not be teaching students to actively receive and listen to that carefully constructed feedback. Too many educators have a professional blind spot when it comes to focusing on the importance of teaching listening skills.

In contrast to the way teaching listening is overlooked, there are dozens and dozens of reading programs. There are beginning-to-read programs, supplemental reading tools, and reading intervention programs. The importance of teaching kids to read cannot be overstated and continues throughout the early grades. But once students enter fourth grade, explicit reading comprehension activities begin to taper and transition more to a content focus. Yet, many students still struggle with reading.

And yet listening is foundational to learning how to read. I'll go into more depth on the connection between listening and reading in a later chapter. Right now, I want to stick with the notion that listening is an important skill that can and should be taught.

Listening didn't come to me without practice and it won't come to your students without practice either. I pride myself on being a good listener. I am a well-trained listener. For 20 years I listened to other people's stories and then retold them on the radio using segments of their voices. You have to be a good listener to have your subjects open up to you and trust you with their stories. And you have to actively listen to ask the right follow-up questions. Sometimes this comes from listening to what's not being said, but what I can hear in their emotions or see in their reactions. I listen closely so that I can hear the main point of the story so that I can understand it well enough to write a news story others will understand.

The majority of what we learn, not just as students but as adults, we learn through listening. There are a variety of studies that cite different percentages of how much we absorb by passively or actively listening, but all of them agree that more than half of what we learn is through our ears. Not our eyes. In the book *Understanding and Developing the Skills of Oral Communication*, the author says 80% of what we learn, we learn by listening.[3]

"Conscious listening creates understanding," says Julian Treasure, a sound and communication expert whose TED talk on listening has been viewed more than 8 million times. While that is a lot of views, his talk on how to speak so that people want to listen has been viewed 28 million times. Epictetus, a Greek philosopher, said "We have two ears and one mouth so that we can listen twice as much as we speak." But it's clear some people like to speak more than listen.

"I think we are much more into speaking than we are into listening. It's the hidden skill, it's the forgotten skill, it's the silent skill. It's easy to ignore," Treasure told me in an interview. Even though he says it's by listening that we can "understand people better. We can be compassionate. And we can live with them, which is very important in a democracy. It's listening that brings connection and understanding."

> *I'm teaching citizenship and when we look at the 14th Amendment and discuss the process of naturalization we play a podcast about whether non-citizens should be allowed to vote in local elections. It leads to a long discussion about the benefits of citizenship and why some people who live legally as residents of the United States might take the extra step of seeking citizenship.*
> —Andrew Garnett-Cook, seventh- and eighth-grade Social Studies teacher, Brookline, MA

When I was a reporter and my stories were heard nationally on NPR, I can't tell you how many times adults told me something they learned by listening to public radio. Sometimes they would cite a fact from one of my stories and not realize it was my report. What people learned from listening would often come up in dinner party conversation. I could see that my friends as well as strangers learn every day by listening to podcasts and public radio. The importance and prevalence of this skill has only grown in the past few years, as the dynamic of information sharing, especially in journalism, has shifted to more audio through podcasts.

Recommended Podcasts for Adults

- News: *The Daily*—an in-depth look at the biggest story of the day anchored on an interview with a reporter from the *New York Times*.

- Science: *Radiolab*—the show uses its subjects and sound design to make you see the world around you differently.

- History: *Throughline*—a show that goes behind the headlines to understand the history of a story.

- Race: *Code Switch*—frank conversations about race with two dynamic hosts and experts in the topics discussed.

- Culture: *Pop Culture Happy Hour*—a casual conversation about pop culture with critics and pop culture experts.

- True Crime: *Crimetown*—a serialized true crime drama that investigates organized crime in various American cities.

Recommended Podcasts for Kids to Get Them Interested in Listening

For ages 5–12:

- Adventure: *Story Pirates*—this show asks a kid for a story and then produces it into a lively audio drama. Also recommended, *The Unexplainable Disappearance of Mars Patel, Eleanor Amplified*, and *The Fina Mendoza Mystery Podcast*.

- Fake News: *The Big Fib*—do you think you can tell fact from fiction? Each episode brings on an expert and a liar and asks a kid to make the call about who is telling the truth.

- Science: *Earth Rangers*—follow Earth Ranger Emma as she explores the natural world. This show takes kids on an audio adventure. Also recommended, *WOW in the World* and *Brains On!*

- Storytelling: *Stories Podcast*—the stories range from retelling of classic fairytales and fables to original stories written and performed by a voice actor. Also recommended, *Circle Round* and *Grim, Grimmer, Grimmest*.

For ages 13–18:

- Crime: *Serial*—a true crime story about a high school student's murder.
- Advice: *Dear Hank and John*—kids will know these brothers (the Greens) from their novels and YouTube channel. They answer teens questions about anything.
- News (sort of): *Wait, Wait, Don't Tell Me*—a quiz show full of humor and news.
- Storytelling: *Welcome to Night Vale*—set in a fake town where strange things happen.
- Teen Voice: *Mic Drop*—from the Canadian Broadcasting Corporation this show gives the mic to tweens and teens to talk about their inner lives and passions.

Remember when you or your parents had glossy magazines delivered to your house on a monthly basis? I learned how to apply blush to highlight my cheekbones by reading *Seventeen*. *Self* magazine showed me how to get flat abs in five weeks. (I never did it.) My mother learned how to cook beef stroganoff from *Gourmet* magazine to impress guests. All of these magazines no longer have print editions. In 1980, more than 62 million Americans got a daily print newspaper. Today, that number has dropped by more than half.[4] News has moved online and more recently into podcasts. So has information about your favorite topics.

> According to one study, "We listen to the equivalent of a book a day; talk the equivalent of a book a week, read the equivalent of a book a month, and write the equivalent of a book a year."[5]

The way we consume information has shifted to listening and viewing. You are more likely to watch a video or listen to a podcast than read a newspaper or magazine to get information. Both require good listening skills. And perhaps if you feel your listening skills could be improved, you, too, can bring a more active and conscious approach to something we often take for granted.

That's why teaching listening as a skill is more important than ever.

Class Activity: Nonverbal Sound

Sound is everywhere, even where you would least expect it. Nonverbal sound conveys a lot of information and complements the text in a podcast. It adds something you just can't get otherwise. Encouraging your students to listen to the nonverbal sounds in the stories listed below is a fun way to engage your students in a conversation about sound and listening. Here are a few suggestions for sound-based stories that will captivate them.

"The Secret Language of Plants"

Did you know plants are making noise as they grow? Corn crackles and hums as it grows. Cacti make noise when touched. The NPR story "Shhhhh. Listen Closely. Your Plants Might be Talking" walks you through an audio tour of an exhibit showing that plants are alive and communicate in their own way. [1] It features children who are drawn to the low rumble and hum of plant growth.

"Fish Sounds"

A marine biologist says listening to fish is key to understanding their behavior. Each fish sounds different. Fish are often making the noises as "advertisement calls" looking for a mate. And they make sounds while breeding. In the WBUR story "How Fish Noises Can Help Manage Species" a scientist is mapping fish sounds because he believes it will make it easier to protect them. [2]

The Sound of Silence

Can we ever find silence? With so many planes, machines, and other man-made sounds, it's become increasingly difficult to find a spot in the United States that is totally devoid of noise. This NPR story, "Are You Listening? Hear What Uninterrupted Silence Sounds Like," takes us to a quiet spot and records the world without any human sounds. [3]

Whale Sounds

In this NPR story, "It Took a Musician's Ear to Decode the Complex Song in Whale Calls," we meet the first marine biologists who discovered that humpback whales sing. [4] It's a haunting call that was discovered with underwater microphones. But the latest discovery is that whales have been changing their songs, making a sort of melody and rhythm.

Elementary School Students: To draw attention to the nonverbal sounds of a story and what they convey, ask students to create a six-column graphic organizer labeled: Who, What, Where, When, Why, How. Play the audio for students, pausing frequently at intervals of approximately 30 seconds to allow students a moment to reflect on the nonverbal sounds they hear. Use the Think-Pair-Share Technique to structure a brief dialogue between students to verbalize what they heard and what it added to the story.[6] This strategy is especially helpful for English language learners (ELs) and Individualized Education Program (IEP) students by giving them a chance to process the task and practice constructing and receiving language related to this thinking task. Students should then jot down notes related to the *who, what,* or *where* aspects of the story and nonverbal sounds they hear. Repeat this process to the end of the story.

Once students have finished, ask them to discuss the ideas in the story related to the *when, why,* and *how* aspects of the characters, setting, challenges faced, and nonverbal sounds used to tell their stories. Once students have had a chance to listen, reflect, and discuss elements of the story, ask them to draw either a collage of images, a sequence of images like those found in a graphic novel, or a single scene that connects the sources of the nonverbal sounds to the characters, setting, and main events that took place.

Middle/High School Students: Following listening to the audio, ask them to answer the prompt: What did the nonverbal sounds in the story add to the narrative?

The audio and additional teaching resources for these stories can also be found at https://listenwise.com/book.

LISTENING MATTERS IN K–12 INSTRUCTION

Listening is the backbone of knowledge. Your students' success will, in part, be determined by their listening skills. Don't believe it? Then reflect on the standards. Most educators know the Common Core changed educational standards across the nation starting in 2009. But many have not embraced listening as one of those changes. In fact, listening appears in all 50 states' English Language Arts (ELA) standards, regardless of whether the state follows the Common Core. By including listening in the standards for a well-rounded education, leaders in the field are saying—listen! This is important to student success. These standards define what students should be capable of by the time they advance through each grade and ultimately go to college or start a career. As of 2020, the Common Core standards are being used by 40 states and the District of Columbia. And 22 states test listening on their standardized tests (see Figure 2.1).

Figure 2.1 Map of states that test listening.
Source: Listenwise.

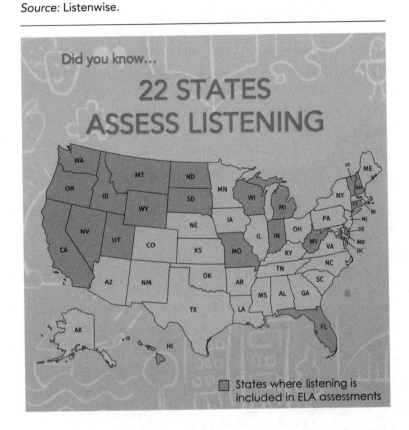

Two of the most influential states with their own listening standards are Florida and Texas. Each takes a different, but more prescriptive approach than the Common Core, when it comes to listening. Florida integrates listening directly with reading by asking students to make comparisons between the two on their high-stakes tests. Anything presented auditorily is considered a "text." Texas considers listening a "foundational language skill" and says students should know how to listen actively. But Texas does not test listening on the State of Texas Assessments of Academic Readiness (STAAR® tests).

Common Core Speaking and Listening Standards

Listening is a College and Career Readiness Anchor Standard of the Common Core

CCSS.ELA-LITERACY.CCRA.SL.2

Integrate and evaluate information presented in diverse media and formats, including visually, quantitatively, and orally.

CCSS.ELA-LITERACY.CCRA.SL.3

Evaluate a speaker's point of view, reasoning, and use of evidence and rhetoric.

(Source: Common Core State Standards Initiative[7])

Florida Reading and Listening Standards

Florida: LAFS.6.RL.3.7—Compare and contrast the experience of reading a story, drama, or poem to listening to or viewing an audio, video, or live version of the text, including contrasting what they "see" and "hear" when reading the text to what they perceive when they listen or watch.

Texas Reading Standards

Texas Essential Knowledge and Skills or TEKS for ELA: 110.6. English Language Arts and Reading, Grade 4, Adopted 2017. (b) Knowledge and skills.

(1) Developing and sustaining foundational language skills: listening, speaking, discussion, and thinking—oral language. The student develops oral language through listening, speaking, and discussion. The student is expected to:

(A) listen actively, ask relevant questions to clarify information, and make pertinent comments

(Source: Florida CPALMS[8] and Texas TEKS[9])

TESTING LISTENING

When the Common Core was introduced, two new standardized tests were created to assess the standards: The Smarter Balanced Assessment Consortium or SBAC and the Partnership for Assessment Readiness for College and Careers or PARCC. States adopted one or the other of these assessments or sought waivers to create their own tests. For instance, Florida uses the Florida Comprehensive Assessment Test or FCAT.

> *Almost all of the other content we use is visual, so it's great to tap into students' listening skills.*
> —Amy Beaucham, gifted and talented teacher, grades 1–5, Fayette County, GA

When the tests were first created, both the SBAC and PARCC assessments had listening questions in the English Language Arts portion of the test. In the PARCC, speaking and listening was field tested in 2015. However, most states requested waivers from the listening portion of the test, citing time constraints and a lack of the required technology. They were granted because measuring listening in large-scale, summative assessments was not a practical option because districts didn't have laptops for every student. Now listening is not routinely tested on the PARCC and the test is rarely used.

The SBAC test is more widely used. Seventeen states are in the consortium, including California, and they all test listening on their high-stakes exams. In addition, states that are not SBAC such as Florida and Indiana have listening passages with questions in the ELA sections of their yearly tests for general education students. As of 2021, 22 states test listening in the ELA portions of their exams (refer to Figure 2.1). In addition, all students who are designated English learners are tested yearly on their listening as part of the classification process.

Why is this important? Because we know that often what is tested drives instruction. If state education leaders do not include listening on their standardized tests, they are shortchanging students. It means they are not holding teachers accountable for teaching the listening standard as a critical skill. And students won't take listening instruction seriously.

Testing listening in many states begins in the third grade and continues every year until the eighth grade. In a smaller number of states listening is tested again in the 10th and 11th grades. We at Listenwise estimate that more than 10 million students from grades 3 to 11 are tested in the United States on their listening skills every year. 10 million! If that many students were tested on their ability to perfectly hard boil an egg, you would bet there would be a lot of practice.

Class Activity: Listening to Background Knowledge

A good listening practice, and one that Listenwise lessons stress, is to always begin teaching listening by first listening to your students. Every standards-aligned lesson has a listening guide that helps you activate student knowledge by inviting them to share what they know about the subject of a story. In this activity, you are modeling good listening skills as well as engaging students in thinking about the subject they are about to hear about.

Upper Elementary Students in Grades 3–5: Use the story "A Status Update And A Fight Against Bullying" to hear about a student whose peers supported her in a unique way when she was bullied. [5]

Open class by telling students they are going to listen to a story about a student who was bullied. Ask students to think about their own experiences with bullies, whether they have been bullied, seen others bullied, or possibly bullied someone else. Next, ask students to describe actions or words a bully might use. Record responses using a three-column list with headings

"Bullying looks like" and "Bullying sounds like" and "What can be done." The list will prepare students to actively listen for evidence of bullying in the story and responses that took place.

You may want students to listen to the audio individually, in pairs, or in groups, pausing to jot down notes indicating where they heard evidence of bullying in the story. When finished, students should discuss where they heard someone in the story do something to respond to bullying. Encourage students to add their own responses for what could be done in similar situations.

Following the audio, ask students to reflect on how the mother of the student who was bullied asked her daughter to consider the bully in the story. Discuss how a bully might feel if a large number of people identified and responded to their actions or words. Could a response to bullying behavior become bullying? Ask students to look back at the "What can be done" column of the chart. Were the responses fair? Would they have embarrassed anyone? This final discussion gives students a chance to extend the story and consider how a response to bullying should balance justice with empathy.

Middle/High School Students: Use the story "The Psychology of a Bully." [6] Bullying is a sensitive subject, so be sure to reiterate your classroom norms before proceeding.

Open class by discussing bullying in general and listening closely to your students and encouraging them to listen to each other. Ask students some foundational questions, especially if this is the first in a series of lessons on bullying for your students: What is bullying? What are some behaviors that bullies exhibit? Why do you think people bully? Where do they learn how to bully? Explore answers to these questions in a class discussion. You may want to raise the question: Do we all have the potential to be a bully? How so? This will get students prepared to address subsequent questions about increasing empathy, building community, and preventing bullying. It will also prepare students to hear an interview with a teenager who was once a bully and was also the victim of a bully.

Following the audio, ask students to reflect on whether they agree or disagree that everyone has the capability of being a bully. Why or why not?

The audio for these stories can also be found at https://listenwise.com/book.

Digital adoption in education has evolved in the past decade. It's transitioned quickly since the coronavirus pandemic forced schools to close and move teaching entirely online. Now, most schools have enough laptops or computers for every student. Many school systems sent Chromebooks home with their students for remote learning. The barriers to testing listening because of a lack of equipment are lifted. And the ability now to use listening exercises and lessons tied to listening is greater than ever because students can listen anywhere, on their laptops, home computers, or phones. Let's look more closely at an example of how students' listening comprehension is tested on the Florida FCAT tests.

Florida Example of a Listening Question

On the eighth-grade ELA practice test, students are asked to listen to a podcast and read a Fact Sheet/FAQ on the same subject: compact fluorescent light bulbs (CFLs). The audio is a brief interview, about a minute and a half, with someone from the Environmental Protection Agency who is not identified. The audio is referred to as Passage 1. Passage 2 is a written document, a Fact Sheet/FAQs on fluorescent lamps. Students are asked to listen to Passage 1 (the audio) and read Passage 2 (the FAQ), synthesize the information, and answer questions on the information combined in both passages.

In the questions directly related to the audio, students are asked to identify the interviewer's purpose and how the interviewer achieves her purpose. Listeners are asked to select two advantages of using audio in the passage to present information about CFLs. One question asks students about several claims made about CFLs and for students to identify which claim is offered without sufficient supporting evidence, using both the audio and the FAQ.

Students are then presented with a chart and told to click the boxes to match the claims made by the speaker in the podcast with the supporting evidence for each claim. This requires students to synthesize the knowledge gained from both listening to and reading about fluorescent light bulbs in the FAQ.

These are advanced skills that students need to be trained to do. Active listening for purpose, evidence, and tone is not something most students can learn on their own. And the skills gained in this kind of practice can be applied across media.

The listening portion of these tests is significant and impacts the overall outcome of students' ELA scores. In many of the state-level tests, listening comprises between 10% and 20% of the overall ELA score. On the California Assessment of Student Performance and Progress or CAASPP listening is one of four scores in the ELA section reported out to districts, schools, and students. Students are assessed on reading, writing, listening, and research/inquiry. California is the largest state to test listening in their general population. Imagine not teaching your math students geometry and expecting them to do well on the tests!

You might be saying to yourself, of course it's not the same as teaching math. Students are listening all the time. This is true, but what are they listening for? Are they listening for specific details, the main idea, or an inference? Have they ever put on headphones, listened to an audio passage, and then answered questions? That's what is required of them on state tests.

The most important outcome of teaching listening skills is successful learners, setting up your students for success in college or a career.

EFFECTIVE LISTENING IN COLLEGE

When I went to college, I remember how surprised I was that classes only met twice a week for long lectures. Coming from a typical high school, I was used to daily classes that were under one hour. My stamina for listening wasn't challenged. Of the 50-minute class period, I probably only needed to listen for about 20 minutes. It was a huge adjustment for me to sit in a two-hour college lecture, pay attention, and listen the entire time. I wasn't prepared.

Today, some classes are streamed live or recorded, so technically students don't have to show up and listen. They can even listen to them multiple times, if necessary. This is time-consuming and many professors, especially in seminars, don't allow recording. Nothing substitutes for a student being present in the classroom, actively listening, asking questions, and engaging with the information. In addition to optimizing the learning opportunity, it's good preparation for a job interview, where they can't stop and replay the employer's questions.

Clearly, the stakes for having good listening skills are higher in college. In any continuing education course students will be confronted with a more challenging listening environment. Some classes have hundreds of students so there will be many distractions. The instructor might speak softly, mumble, or speak with a heavy accent. Students will need to adapt their listening or take more cues from what's written on the board. The emphasis, and the burden, on listening and learning is almost entirely on students.

Effective listening is essential to undergraduate success. Numerous studies speak to the importance of listening for success in college. One study gave 400 freshman college students a listening test at the beginning of their first semester. They were given no listening instruction during the semester, but went about their academics normally. At the end of their freshman year, researchers found nearly 69% of the freshmen who scored high on the listening test were honor students at the end of the year. Of the students who scored poorly on the listening test, 49% were on academic probation.[10] This study makes a strong case for improving students' listening skills to prepare them for college.

Another study in the *Imperial Journal of Interdisciplinary Research* found that good listening habits determine the academic accomplishments of students to a great extent.[11] Just Google "college success and listening," and you'll find that universities are helping students prepare for success by teaching them about listening. Dartmouth College in New Hampshire has a section under "Academic Skills Center" that lists the 10 Bad Habits of Listening and How to Turn Them Around. Another list is called Learning by Listening. Elizabethtown College in Pennsylvania has a Learning Zone website dedicated to students' academic success that includes a module on listening skills.[12] Why would colleges place such an emphasis on listening skills if they weren't critical for success?

However, this focus on listening appears to be strictly in study guides and online preparation materials. Colleges rarely teach good listening skills. Even in communications courses, little time is devoted to honing listening skills. Maybe because of this lack of formal listening instruction, students don't know they can control and improve their listening skills.

The transition from high school to college is a difficult one. Students are bombarded with the "new." New town, new roommate, new classes. They can be ready with their "old" skills to succeed. You have the ability to arm your students with the listening habits they need to excel, starting as early as kindergarten and all the way through senior year. It is in your power.

VALUED LISTENING AT WORK

Let's jump ahead in your students' lives. They have graduated from high school, maybe attended college. Irrespective of their level of postsecondary education, they will need good listening skills.

Why? Because most jobs require them. In the workforce, students' understanding won't be scaffolded with graphic organizers and adapted texts. They will most likely learn their jobs through oral communication. It could be a training video, in-person instruction, or in a meeting with their new boss. They will be told what to do and potentially shown in a shadow or mentor program. To onboard more quickly and begin putting their skills to good use, they will need great listening skills and some strategies for absorbing the information.

Today's interconnected world puts communication skills at the top of the list for career readiness. A report by the Graduate Management Admission Council shows that of the five top-ranked skills, four are communications-related, and number two is listening.[13]

The ability to listen, speak clearly, and write well are the attributes of the most successful employees. A hiring study by Google found that the seven top characteristics of successful employees at Google are all soft skills, including communicating and listening well.[14] Another study found that business leaders and academics listed listening as one of the most important skills for an effective professional, yet only 1.5% of articles in business journals dealt with listening effectiveness.[15]

In one of the most widely read management books, *The Seven Habits of Highly Effective People*, author Stephen Covey says "most people do not listen with the intent to understand; they listen with the intent to reply."[16]

An adviser to the CEOs of some of the world's biggest corporations wrote in the *Harvard Business Review* that listening deficits can "paralyze cross-unit collaboration, sink careers, and potentially derail the company."[17] Listening doesn't only benefit leaders. Good listening helps coworkers collaborate more effectively. For example, if you actively listen to your colleague the first time she shows you how to do a project, you'll have fewer questions and your work will be higher-quality than if you only half-listened, which will save you both time and energy. And your colleague will think more highly of you because you only needed to be told once. Don't you already feel that way about some students who listen and respond the first time they are told to take out their books or put away their cell phones? In your classroom, what behavior do you see when you stop and give your full attention to a student and listen to them?

Effective leaders know that listening is integral to any relationship. But I would argue it's critical to building a company. I have created a company around building listening skills so it only makes sense that listening is one of our core values at Listenwise.

LISTENWISE CORE VALUES

We care about listening.

- We listen to each other.
- We listen to our customers.
- We listen to the data.

First, let's pull apart listening to each other. That's not just about nodding your head in a meeting while someone else is talking. In our company it means everyone's input is valued. I know someone has listened to me when they follow-up a meeting with an email confirming or elaborating on what I said.

We listen to our customers every day. We reply quickly to inquiries. We conduct trainings and respond to problems. But listening shouldn't only be passive. We ask our customers about their experiences with Listenwise and how they use it with students. We don't just listen to the good things that teachers say about Listenwise. Nor do we only listen when there is a problem we need to address. Listening to teachers is a fundamental part of what we do.

I know data doesn't "talk." But data can tell a story, and if you are not listening to that story, you could be missing a major point. In our company, we know that listening to teachers sometimes only tells part of the story. We also look at usage patterns, the number of times a podcast is played, and the frequency of a quiz being assigned. These data points also guide us to improve Listenwise. We reflect on these core values together periodically and discuss how we are living up to them and where we can improve.

These core values could just as well be adapted for your classrooms with some minor adaptations, which I invite you to create in the Reflections at the end of this chapter.

Engaging your students in a discussion about listening as a skill and how your classroom could become a model listening class is the first step to teaching listening as a skill. And teaching active listening will set your students up for college and career success.

PERSONAL RELATIONSHIPS ARE STRENGTHENED BY LISTENING

I would be remiss if I didn't talk about how listening is critical in personal relationships. I think we all know that if you listen to your partner, you have a better relationship. And if you listen to your friends and children, you will also be rewarded. If you want your personal relationships to be healthy, being able to listen is key. The chances of miscommunicating drop when you give someone your attention, listen objectively, and show that you understand by paraphrasing what he or she has said.

Active listening is also crucial as a parent. When you show your children that you're truly concentrating on them, they'll feel supported and loved—which is the foundation for an open, trusting relationship. I know this as a parent of two teenage girls. But it's nice to see it confirmed by the Center for Parenting Education. The organization says that "active listening is the single most important skill you can have in your parenting toolbelt."[18]

We demonstrate active listening in my family at the dinner table. I learned early on that just calling the kids to the table for "family dinner" wasn't enough. When they were young, the dinner conversation was unstructured and meandered. It was not always clear who was supposed to be talking and what constituted good listening. When the kids were in elementary school, we started a new dinner table tradition focused on a few key questions.

At the time I started the ritual of asking the same questions at every meal, I didn't know much about the importance of building listening skills. But I was a reporter and I knew the key to communication was asking good questions. What I learned through my own family practice, was that building solid, empathetic listening skills takes modeling, time, and patience.

Listening at the Dinner Table
How was your day?
Tell me one thing that happened that was good.
Tell me one thing that happened that was bad.
What did you do that was nice for someone else?

By starting with an easy question that can be answered in one or two words, such as "How was your day?" my children felt at ease. And by using the same questions every meal, they knew what to expect. It can be easy to sum up the day with one word, such as "Okay." This is good as a conversation opener; it's warming them up. The next question is the more important one. By asking someone to tell you one good thing that happened to them today, you are asking them to tell you a story. You signify you are open to listening to them. And you are asking them to be specific and detailed, not just list things that happened. You are inviting them to go in depth. You don't know whether the story will be long or short. You aren't telling them how to respond. It's up to them. You should be all ears and ask many follow-up questions.

Wrapping up the person's "turn" by asking them a short self-reflective question about themselves and the impact they have on others and the world around them turns the conversation outward. We always ask, "What did you do that was nice for someone else?" We, as parents, want to listen to and learn from our children about how they are impacting the world. Each person at the dinner table is asked these four questions at almost every dinner we have around the table. And if you are a visitor to our table, you will be asked them, and listened to, as well.

Listening to Difficult Stories

As a reporter I have often been challenged as a listener as I covered stories that were difficult to hear. I listened to mothers who lost their children to an opioid drug overdose. I listened to adult men speak for the first time about the sexual abuse they suffered by Catholic priests. And I listened into the personal story of a family whose father had been deployed to Iraq in 2006.

My series, "War on the Homefront," chronicled what it was like for the Scanlon family to adjust to life without their father as he served a National Guard deployment to Iraq for 15 months. I visited and interviewed them frequently over the time he was away, listening to intimate phone conversations and frustrating parenting moments. Many of my reports, including "National Guard Family Adjusts to Deployment," [7] were heard on NPR.

Even though my husband and I model good listening at the dinner table, I admit I had one daughter whose listening skills needed some improvement. She was only listening for when your story ended so she could tell hers. You could sense it. I pointed this out to her and she admitted she was just waiting for her turn to talk.

What worked to turn her around was to mimic her behavior when she was telling a story. I interrupted a few times because I wanted to comment and clearly showed I wasn't listening.

As soon as she finished, I didn't ask any follow-up questions, but just started my story. She complained that I was a bad listener. She didn't feel heard, and it wasn't a good feeling. Lesson learned. It's a tactic we've had to practice at the dining room table several times, because old habits are hard to break. It doesn't matter whom you're interacting with: your students, your coworkers, your boss, your friends, your partner, or your kids—active listening is important in every relationship and setting in your life.

And it's vital. According to Julian Treasure, "If you can engage children on the why of listening on a reasonably advanced level, they would understand it creates kindness, people are nice to each other." In other words, listening can create a kinder and more understanding classroom and world.

REFLECTION AND PLANNING

Take this opportunity to write some reflections and plans for action.

How do you demonstrate/model good listening skills in your classroom?

_____

_____

What are the first steps you could take to help your students understand the importance of listening?

_____

_____

What are your classroom's core values around listening?

_____

_____

Audio Resources

[1] Cronin, D. (2019, August 25). Shhhhh. Listen closely. Your plants might be talking. NPR, www.npr.org/2019/ 08/25/753208704/shhhhh-listen-closely-your-plants-might-be-talking.

[2] Ahmed, B. (2012, May 16). How fish noises can help manage species. WBUR, www.wbur.org/news/2012/05/16/fish-sounds.

[3] Patel, S.S. (2018, August 10). Are you listening? Hear what uninterrupted silence sounds like. NPR, www.npr.org/2018/08/10/633201540/are-you-listening-hear-what-uninterrupted-silence-sounds-like.

[4] McQuay, B., and Joyce, C. (2015, August 6). It took a musician's ear to decode the complex song in whale calls. NPR, www.npr.org/2015/08/06/427851306/it-took-a-musicians-ear-to-decode-the-complex-song-in-whale-calls.

[5] Chakrabarti, Meghna. (2012, November 2). A status update and a fight against bullying. *Radio Boston*, WBUR, www.wbur.org/radioboston/2012/11/02/pigtail-bullying.

[6] SanGiovanni, Iris. (2011, November). Psychology of a bully. *PRX*, beta.prx.org/stories/73045-psychology-of-a-bully.

[7] Brady-Myerov, Monica. (2006, November 30). National Guard family adjusts to deployment. NPR, www.npr.org/templates/story/story.php?storyId=6561774.

References

1. Hogan, T., Adlof, S.M., & Alonzo, C.N. (2014). On the importance of listening comprehension. *International Journal of Speech-Language Pathology, 16*(3): 199–207.

2. Beall, M.L., Gill-Rosier, J., Tate, J., & Matten, A. (2008). State of the context: Listening in education. *International Journal of Listening, 22*(2), 123–132. doi:10.1080/10904010802174826.

3. Hunsaker, R.A. (1990). *Understanding & developing the skills of oral communication: Speaking & listening.* Englewood, CO: Morton.

4. Watson, A. (2020, March 3). Number of daily newspapers in the United States from 1970 to 2018. https://www.statista.com/

statistics/183408/number-of-us-daily-newspapers-since-1975/
(accessed September 10, 2020).

5. Buckley, M. (1992). Focus on research: We listen to a book a day; we speak a book a month: Learning from Walter Loban, *Language Arts* 69, 622–626.

6. Simon, Kathy Allen. Using the Think-Pair-Share Technique. ReadWriteThink, www.readwritethink.org/professional-development/strategy-guides/using-think-pair-share-30626.html.

7. Common Core State Standards Initiative. (n.d.). English language arts standards. "College and Career Readiness Anchor Standards for Speaking and Listening" http://www.corestandards.org/ELA-Literacy/CCRA/SL/1/ (accessed September 22, 2020).

8. State of Florida. (2020). LAFS.6.RL.3.7. https://www.cpalms.org/Public/PreviewStandard/Preview/5950 (accessed September 10, 2020).

9. State of Texas. (2020). 19 TAC Chapter 110. Texas essential knowledge and skills for English language arts and reading. http://ritter.tea.state.tx.us/rules/tac/chapter110/ch110a.html (accessed September 10, 2020).

10. Conaway, M.S. (1982). Listening: Learning tool and retention agent. In Algier, A.S. and Algier, K.W. (Eds.), *Improving reading and study skills*. San Francisco: Jossey-Bass. [Google Scholar]

11. Shali, S.K. (2017). The power of listening ability and its effects on academic performance: An examination of college students. *Imperial Journal of Interdisciplinary Research, 3*.

12. Learning Zone. (n.d.). https://www.etown.edu/offices/learning/Module_4_Listening_Skills.aspx (accessed September 25, 2020).

13. Graduate Management Admission Council. (2017). *Corporate Recruiters Survey Report 2017*. www.gmac.com/-/media/files/gmac/research/employment-outlook/2017-gmac-corporate-recruiters-web-release.pdf.

14. Strauss, V. (2019, April 5). Analysis | The surprising thing Google learned about its employees—and what it means for today's students. *Washington Post*, https://www.washingtonpost.com/news/answer-sheet/wp/2017/12/20/the-surprising-thing-google-learned-about-its-employees-and-what-it-means-for-todays-students/ (accessed September 11, 2020).

15. Smeltzer, L.R. (1993). Emerging questions and research paradigms in business communication research. *Journal of Business Communication, 30*(2) 181–198.

16. Covey, S.R. (2004). *The 7 habits of highly effective people: Powerful lessons in personal change.* New York, NY: Free Press.

17. Charan, R. (2014, July 23). The Discipline of Listening. *Harvard Business Review*, https://hbr.org/2012/06/the-discipline-of-listening (accessed September 29, 2020).

18. The Skill of Active Listening. (n.d.). Center for Parenting Education, https://centerforparentingeducation.org/library-of-articles/healthy-communication/the-skill-of-listening/ (accessed September 11, 2020).

Chapter 3

This Is Your Brain on Listening

It was a long day at work. And an even longer commute home.

Vicki Beck's class went on a field trip to the Museum of Science. Justin forgot his permission slip for the field trip, and she had to chase down his mother. Right before the bus left for the trip to the science museum, Clara felt sick to her stomach and ran to the nurse's office. And, of course, the trip to the museum was chaotic, with students wandering off to look at the full-size Tyrannosaurus Rex model instead of listening and following instructions.

On the way home, her normally quiet route was blocked with construction on a water main break. At least she had NPR on the radio to keep her occupied.

But now that she's home, in her driveway, 20 minutes later than expected, she can't get out of the car. She is listening to an enthralling story about Ned, a 28-year-old quadriplegic man with severe brain damage who is helped with his daily activities by a monkey. [1]

She can hear the monkey's chirps and whistles in reply to instructions from Ned, whose speech is slow and slurred. Ned is hard for her to understand, but the monkey listens and understands everything he says. They clearly have formed a special connection, maybe even a special language.

She is riveted to the driver's seat of her car listening with her whole body to the sounds the monkey uses to communicate with Ned. She could see this young man smiling as he watches his monkey fetching him a bottle of water from the refrigerator. She couldn't stop listening, she had to hear the end of the story. Even though it has been a very long day, she sits in her car in her driveway to hear the end of the story. And she cries.

"If I could get my students to feel what I just felt listening to this story when I am teaching them something new, they will not forget what they heard," thought Vicki.

TRANSPORTING: HOW HEARING/ LISTENING WORKS

Good audio storytelling has the power to captivate and transport you to another place. It has the power to shape your brain and memory and make you feel more connected to the world. You can bring this power to your class to enhance your teaching and your students' learning. And it's easy and fun for everyone. And it all starts with hearing.

Hearing is a universal sense, according to Seth Horowitz, a neuroscientist at Brown University. Humans have five basic senses: touch, sight, hearing, smell, and taste. But hearing, says Horowitz, "is one of the most basic and universal sensory systems that any earthly organism can have."[1] Why is it so important? It alerts us to the world around us, giving us pleasure or warnings. It never shuts off. It's faster than any of our other senses.

Researchers have found that early vertebrates from 300 million years ago could hear, despite the fact that they hadn't yet developed middle or outer ears. But salamanders could detect sound waves through the vibration of the air.[2] Sound is the basis for all communication in the animal world and even among plants. Hearing happens all the time—out of sight of the source of sound, in the dark, even while we sleep. We are always listening. Hearing is an essential part of communication.

Our ears are amazing. They are engineered to capture the waves that our brains convert into sound and your mind translates into meaning. Hearing is the process by which our body turns sound waves in the air into electrical signals, which our auditory nerve then sends to the brain.[3] "The Journey of Sound to the Brain" video by the National Institutes of Health (NIH) is a brief and fascinating overview of how sound waves get transported to the brain.[4] It's a cartoon depiction about how sound travels through the ear canal to the ear drum. The drum vibrates, which then vibrates three tiny bones. The bones increase the vibrations and send them to the cochlea. It's filled with fluid, which ripples with waves. The hair cells inside the cochlea are moved by the waves and they are turned into electrical signals. Ions rush into the top of the hair cells, which cause the release of chemicals at the bottom of the hair cells. Those neurotransmitters bind to the auditory nerve to create an electrical signal to the brain. The brain interprets the messages as sounds.

Hearing begins in utero. While we develop ears in the second trimester, it's not until the third trimester that our ears connect with our brains.[5] The auditory system continues to develop, and by 28 weeks of gestational age, a fetus can really hear and learn, according to one study, during the last trimester of pregnancy. A fetus has developed "short-term auditory memory" and is hearing outside conversation.[6] Remember, we are floating in amniotic fluid, so what we are hearing is muffled by uterine waters. While you can hear things like your mother's heartbeat, speaking, and music, it's not very clear.

Two to three children out of every 1,000 in the United States are born with hearing loss, according to the NIH.[7] And because hearing and listening are essential to learning how to speak, doctors screen newborn babies within the first month, for their hearing. But that doesn't mean they catch every problem, because hearing loss can happen at any time.

We take our hearing for granted. I know I do. When I had my first child, she was born at full term and passed all the newborn screening tests, including hearing. I never thought about her hearing again as she was developing into a bright and curious toddler. She responded when spoken to and was learning to speak at the right developmental age. Nothing seemed out of the ordinary.

When she was three and a half she was speaking fluently when a friend of mine came to visit. She commented on how my daughter's pronunciation of some words sounded as if she was hard of hearing. As this was my first child, I thought the strange way she said *sun* and *shine* was a kind of baby talk. But my friend's mother was a speech therapist and she recognized the lateral way my daughter said "s." It was similar to how a deaf person speaks.

A lateral lisp is when air is forced over the tongue instead of out the front of the mouth and it makes the "s" and "sh" sound slushy.

My friend and I quickly devised a hearing test. I stood behind my daughter at the dining room table and said in a normal voice to her "Do you want some ice cream?" She did not respond. My friend stood in front of her and said the same thing. She replied with enthusiasm, "Yes!" It was the first step to diagnosing a correctable hearing problem. She had moderate hearing loss due to fluid in her ears. Once officially diagnosed, it was fairly simple to correct by placing tubes in her ears to drain the fluid. Her lisp and incorrect pronunciation of some words took speech therapy and a lot of practice to correct.

Sensory Experience

Simply getting sound to the brain is only part of the magic of listening. Your brain must translate that sound into meaning. And that's where it gets even more complicated. Translating sound waves into meaning engages the auditory regions of the brain. Benjamin Bergen, a cognitive scientist from the University of California in San Diego, writes extensively about how the brain interprets meaning from sounds. He studies how the brain creates mental imagery of what you hear. He explores the embodied simulation hypothesis, which, he writes in his book *Louder than Words*, means "we understand language by simulating in our minds what it would be like to experience the things that the language describes."[8]

People are activating systems in their brain that are responsible for sight, sound, motor control, and olfaction while they are listening to language. He told me in an interview that when you listen to language about action, "about people walking upstairs or opening a can of tuna . . . you activate parts of your brain that actually drive those very actions, motor parts of your brain." In brain imaging studies, the same parts of your brain that actually experience things by directly interacting with the world, such as your visual cortex when you see a bird, also light up when you hear a story about a bird.

For example, you hear a story about a chef who's cooking a delicious meal, frying up garlic for a pasta sauce. You might hear it sizzling and popping in the pan. This story wouldn't just stimulate your language processing areas, it would also stimulate your olfactory and gustatory cortices. You would smell the aromatic garlic and might get hungry. Multiple areas of the brain are engaged. Or if it's a story about a pitcher and a catcher, your brain is sending signals to your motor system and it "lights up" to catch the ball. Language about action triggers motor simulation. Essentially, the whole body gets involved in listening to stories about actions. In other words, your brain sees what it hears in "the mind's eye"—this is what's called auditory scene analysis. This research comes primarily from Bergen, who has done studies using brain scans while subjects are listening or reading.

The associations appear to be more powerful when listening than when reading, says Bergen. "Writing is a very recent invention," Bergen told me and is not a natural or universal phenomenon. But your brain is hardwired to react to sound. Bergen says one study shows that when reading, "your eyes are busy looking at the page, and you are actively seeking out information that flows through your visual system, and if you interfere with that, you are not going to be able to . . . see what the next word is." So your vision system can't create visuals in your mind's eye for the language without interfering with the reading process.

"We imagine sounds using the same brain regions that allow us to hear real sounds," says Bergen.[9] But this connection is made stronger when the message is delivered in a story. People respond in a very immersed way to narratives, to a degree that they don't to declarative description of states of affairs," Bergen told me.

> *Engaging middle school students in the world around them and helping them to understand the perspective of others is a fundamental aspect of their learning. In order to do this, students need to learn to listen. Human voice and story need to be a key element in this learning.*
> —Tracy Sockalosky, middle school teacher,
> Natick, MA

Humans are wired to listen to stories. After all, we've been sharing them since even before we could speak. The earliest rock art was discovered to be 44,000 years old in a cave in Indonesia. In red pigment, cave dwellers drew a story about animals and supernatural people possibly hunting the animals.[10] While there's no way to know if early humans narrated their stories while they drew them on cave walls, they certainly told stories with pictures. Once we humans learned how to speak, oral communication was the primary way to convey information, share knowledge, and express ourselves.

Listening to Stories

Storytelling was the first form of teaching. Cognitive psychologists define teaching as "a behavior in which one animal intends that another learn some skill or acquire some bit of information or knowledge that it did not have previously."[11] In the earliest hunter gatherer societies, there is evidence that humans, for their survival, shared information with each other. This, some believe, is evidence that oral storytelling as pedagogy began in forager societies.[12]

We've come a long way since our foraging days, but our love of and dependence on storytelling hasn't changed much. Paul Zak, a neuroeconomist, found that subjects watching or listening to a dramatic narrative were found to have an increase in cortisol and oxytocin. Cortisol helps the body respond to stress, and oxytocin plays a role in social bonding. Zak found the increase in oxytocin inspired this group to be more empathic to the main characters in the story. The control group, which watched a nondramatic narrative about the same characters, didn't have an increase in oxytocin or cortisol and didn't report feeling empathy.[13]

In your classroom, building empathy is critical to the social and emotional learning of your students. We'll talk more about how listening builds empathy later in this chapter. So why do we love to listen to stories so much? When information is given to us as a straightforward list of facts and figures, two main parts of your brain light up: Broca's area and Wernicke's area (Figure 3.1). These regions handle language processing.

However, when we receive information in a story format, not only are Broca's area and Wernicke's area activated, but the other parts of our brain that deal with the relevant sensory experiences are turned on as well.[15]

Why is this important in your teaching? It means listening to good stories is an extremely powerful way to learn because it engages so many parts of the brain.

There are two relevant takeaways from this scientific research. First, listening to stories is a full-brain workout—except this

Figure 3.1 Diagram of brain highlighting Broca's and Wernicke's areas.
Source: WikiMedia Commons.[14]

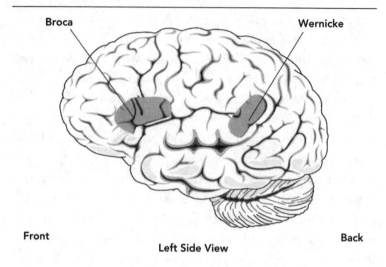

Broca

Wernicke

Front

Back

Left Side View

is one workout that's super enjoyable. Second, it's much easier to remember a narrative than a more straightforward lecture because so much of your brain is engaged with the story.

Class Activity: Sensory Listening

Having your students experience what I call sensory listening is an excellent way to help them understand the neuroscience of what's happening in our brains when we listen. Listen to the NPR story called "Why Killer Viruses Are on the Rise." [2] You will only be playing the first two minutes of the story so it's appropriate for all grade levels. The purpose of listening is to immerse your students in a sensory experience, not focus on the facts and content.

This story takes you to Southeast Asia to find the origins of viruses. The story itself is a complex science story that describes how animals can trigger serious viruses such as the coronavirus or Ebola. The story aired before the COVID-19 pandemic but is relevant to the transmission of that virus. The story begins with the reporter trekking through a thick forest in Borneo with a researcher. The sound effects of hacking through deep underbrush really give your brain a vivid picture. You are walking with them. Maybe you see the dense greenery, smell the moist undergrowth, and feel the prickly thorns on your skin. The scientist talks through the experiment as they are doing it. You are there. The narrative quality is engaging and draws you into the scene.

Stop the audio at 2:15 as they head off to find the bat nets. This is enough of the story to give your students a rich sensory experience. Ask them the following questions:

- What color is the forest?
- Describe the area they are walking though. What sounds give you clues?
- What does the forest smell like? Is it hot or cold in the forest?
- How is the reporter feeling?
- Are there bugs in the forest? How do you know this?
- How big was the roly poly bug? What objects was it compared to?

Point out that each person has a different visual in their minds because they each bring different background knowledge of what a forest looks like, and they are making their own movies in their minds. Discuss why this experience might improve their ability to recall information from the story.

TRANSFIXING: LISTENING AND MEMORY

You may be thinking that being a good listener also means you have a good memory. The book *Moonwalking with Einstein* by Joshua Foer explores memory in depth and concludes that making mental visual images and connecting them along imaginary spatial pathways is a very effective way to remember something.[16] He attends the U.S. Memory Championship and studies how the "mental athletes" or expert memorizers do it. One study shows that the champion memorizers turned the information they were learning, either written or auditory, into images. They engaged their visual memory as well as spatial navigation. They would take a fact and convert it into a picture and place that picture along a spatial path, thus connecting their memories. Your brain is already hardwired to do this while listening, you just need to engage your students with memorable, visual audio.

> *Once they start talking with each other about what it was that they've just heard, there's no other topic that they are discussing. It's not like "what are you going to wear to prom?" It is just absolutely on what they've just heard. I think the amount of effort they're putting in says something about the engagement that they're feeling about it.*
> —Mike Messner, high school Social Studies teacher, Los Altos, CA

You, as a teacher, don't want to just cram facts into the brains of your students. You want them to be able to draw on facts to be critical thinkers who can apply what they know to the world. But it begins with knowing a lot about the world.

One study shows what is widely known in education—background knowledge is key to understanding new information.[17] Two groups of study participants were given the same detailed written account of a half inning of baseball. One group was made up of avid baseball fans, and the other knew far less about baseball. When they were asked to recall what they read about the inning, those with more knowledge of baseball could recount details of the game. Those with little knowledge of baseball remembered unimportant details. Comprehension was better among those with background knowledge, even if they were lower level readers.

Foer concludes "Without a conceptual framework in which to embed what they were learning, they were effectively amnesiacs." Essentially, he says, "the more you know, the easier it is to know more."

If you are a fan of public radio, I am going to guess there was a time in your life when you had a "driveway moment." You probably didn't know you were having a driveway moment, but like Vicki, who couldn't get out of her car until she heard the end of the story about Ned and his monkey, you had to finish listening to a really good story before leaving the car.

"Driveway moment" is public radio lingo for a transfixing story that glues you to the story emotionally. As a veteran public radio reporter, I aspired to create those moments. My goal was to capture emotional audio, write vivid scenes, and put it all together in a compelling narrative. I didn't always meet the high standards I set for myself, but I tried.

What I didn't know as a reporter was that the driveway moment is really a concept cognitive scientists call the "immersed experiencer view."[18] It means that understanding language is akin in some way to actually being there and experiencing the events the language describes. Not all researchers agree, but there is evidence showing that people are simulating what it would be like to "be there" in a scene.[19] This makes sense when you think about the neuroscience involved—your brain is making a movie, including the sights and smells of what it's hearing. Researchers have even shown that your perception of the events is from the perspective of the storyteller.

Transfixing Audio

These are some of the stories I wrote for WBUR that I hope will glue you to your seat and make you feel something. They demonstrate how sound can transport and transfix. These stories can only be found at www.monicabradymyerov.com.

The Threshold Choir is a story about a volunteer choir that visits patients in hospice who are near death. The sound of songs eases the transition to death. The emotion comes through.

Hearing the last chirps and squeaks of a dying whale is profoundly moving. The story, Beached Whales, chronicles volunteers trying to save a pod of beached whales on Cape Cod. It focuses on one whale and his dying moments.

A simple camping trip turns into a battle against the elements in this story about Grape Island in the Boston Harbor. The rumble of thunder and the pounding of rain put you on the island, hoping to stay dry under the tarp.

A study conducted by Rolf Zwaan and his colleagues tested this idea that you are really seeing and experiencing things you hear by mentally representing them in dynamic simulations. Zwaan had 82 people listen to sentences about motions but from different perspectives. In one case, the sentence was "The pitcher hurled the softball to you." Zwaan was testing to see if, in hearing this sentence, you would be mentally putting yourself at home plate, with a bat in hand and "seeing" the ball getting larger as it rapidly approached. The other sentence was "You hurled the softball to the pitcher." Would your mind's eye see this sentence as a ball quickly getting smaller as you threw it to the pitcher?[20]

The answer was yes. Participants more quickly categorized the pictures of the softball when they appeared to be moving in the same direction as the sentence depicted. In other words, if you heard the sentence "The pitcher hurled the softball to you" participants were slightly faster recognizing two pictures in rapid succession of a softball that was getting slightly larger.

As a teacher, helping students experience others' perspectives develops valuable skills. Being "in the shoes" of another person can transform learning about an historical event or a character in literature into a deep and meaningful experience. This research shows that using oral communication alters the listener's perception. While the softball study was only focused on the movement of a ball, Benjamin Bergen shows that "language does manipulate what perspective you adopted when you mentally simulate objects."

Bergen conducted a study in which participants heard or read about static objects. One sentence was "Through the clean goggles, the skier could easily identify the moose." The other sentence was "Through the fogged goggles, the skier could hardly identify the moose." Then they were shown a picture of a moose. Similar to the softball study, people had more trouble "seeing" the moose picture if they had read or heard the sentence with the perspective of the foggy goggles.

Bergen concludes that we mentally simulate objects and events from the perspective of someone actually experiencing the scene.[21]

Over the years of leading Listenwise, I have heard many teachers express this exact concept to me when using an audio story with their students. They can see their students adopt the perspective of the people in the story. Their students tell them that listening to a story makes them feel like they are part of the story.

Class Activity: Audio Immersive Experiences

Elementary/Middle School Students: A good example of "in your shoes" listening is the NPR story "Traveling Exhibit Shows What It's Like to be a Refugee." [3] It's an exhibit that helps you walk in the shoes of refugees. You are immediately put in the position of a refugee—the reporter referring to the listener as "you" and "we." You are given 30 seconds to select five items that you will take as you are forced to flee your home. As visitors go through the exercise of getting robbed or paying off smugglers, they must lose some of their five items. You can hear a visitor's voice saying "It feels too real now . . . I want to go home, not here." You never see the people in the exercise, but you feel their emotions.

Play entire story until 3:55.

Ask students: How did this story make you feel? How did the visitors to the exhibit react to the refugee simulation? What part of the story made you feel anxious or unhappy? What would you take if you had to leave your home within five minutes?

High School Students: A good example of a story that helps students put themselves in the shoes of others is "The Little Rock Nine." [4] It takes listeners back to 1957 and the desegregation of Little Rock Central High School in Arkansas. The story follows the nine African American students who were the first brave teens to attend the school on the first day of integration. When they arrived at the school they were pushed and jeered at, and one was hit by a brick. You can hear the angry crowd in the story and the insistent questioning of a reporter. The black students remain eerily silent in the audio.

Play the first 1:50 of the story.

Ask students: How did the crowd sound? How did the students sound? How do you think the black students felt walking through the angry crowd? What would you do if you were in their situation?

Full lessons and audio for both of these stories can also be found at https://listenwise.com/book.

In a classroom, you are constrained by the walls of the school. Even in remote learning, there aren't many opportunities for your students to experience something authentic. That's why using audio can be so transformative. It can drop those walls, telescope the distance, and bring the outside in.

You may be thinking, video does that as well. It's true that video creates a more complete visual picture of an event. But it only establishes one perspective, that of the videographer or photographer. And the visuals are delivered to viewers to interpret, not to imagine. Sound in videos is also usually less engaging and intimate. Videographers don't think about capturing sound to tell a story in the same way that audio engineers do. Reporters who focus only on audio know they need to really listen to their surroundings because hearing crickets in the night will set a scene. Or recording the crunch of biting into an apple will be the perfect sound to start a story about a new varietal of apple.

I liked the podcast because it gives first person P.O.V. on a topic by the author so I am able to really understand what I am learning.
—11th-grade student, Boston, MA

It may sound counterintuitive, but sound is visual. And as science shows, it requires more from your brain to create the picture that accompanies the sounds. It forces your students to draw on what they already know to create that mental image. Encouraging students to pull from their background knowledge is essential in learning. And it can make a deeper and more lasting impact because it has meaning for them. Or it can spark an emotion that imprints on them. It can make them feel something.

One study shows that dramatization in storytelling is also important in engaging the listener's imagination.[22] This is no surprise to anyone who has listened to the podcast Serial. The episodic telling of the murder of a high school student by her ex-boyfriend is one of the most popular podcasts and exploded the podcast genre into the mainstream.

The first-person narrator sounds like she's talking to you and pulls you into the story and its many twists as she shares how her thinking about the murder evolved. It stimulates your imagination. This is not your "voice of God" narrator.

Emma Rodero, a communications and psychology professor who studies how audio and radio affect attention and memory, believes that listening requires more from your brain. After all, when you're listening to a story, rather than reading it, you must process the information at the same rate it's being presented. She told *The Atlantic*, "Audio is one of the most intimate forms of media because you are constantly building your own images of the story in your mind and you're creating your own production . . . And that, of course, is something that you can never get with visual media."[23] Rodero's work also found listening to dramatic telling of stories paints more vivid pictures.[24]

TRANSFORMING: LISTENING AND EMOTIONS

Sound signals are routed to parts of the brain that deal with basic functions—sound drives emotion, according to neuroscientist Seth Horowitz. "Sounds are among the most common and powerful stimuli for emotions."[25] For primates, hearing is the most important sense because it can alert us to danger. You can process sounds in hundredths of seconds or less. There is no time to put up emotional barriers or think about how you feel when you hear something, you just feel and react. And studies have shown that the sounds that make you feel the strongest are human voices.[26] A loud crash may make you jump in your seat, but the sound of someone whispering a secret to a friend will make you sit up and listen.

Horowitz says that "any communication is about first evoking an emotional response on the part of the listener." And the emotional basis of listening is not about the words, but about how we speak, known as prosody. It means focusing on the oral language that is not words but tone, volume, rhythm, and intimation. You might not speak Italian, but if you heard an Italian mother yelling at her son for tipping over her pot of tomato sauce, you could infer what she was saying. You would understand the emotion of her speech even if you didn't understand the words.

I think we overlook the importance of prosody in our own mother tongue. It washes over us in all the communication we absorb. We don't ask ourselves or our students to stop and listen for the emotional meaning behind the words. And our students aren't often asked to do that because they are so often communicating by text on their cell phones, where prosody is entirely missing.

A Common Sense Media survey in 2018 asked teens how they preferred to communicate with their friends.[27] Texting won out with 35% of teens saying they preferred to text rather than speak (32%). But what's disturbing from a listening perspective is that in 2012, when they first asked teens that question, the majority, 49%, said they preferred speaking in person to their friends. That means there's been a significant loss of listening time.

This can have an impact on social and emotional learning. Ask your students if they are familiar with the phrase "tone deaf." Explain that while it can be a way to describe someone who can't hold a tune in music, it's also an expression used to describe people who don't hear the emotional content of someone's words.

Class Activity: Practicing Prosody

Select a word or phrase for your students to say in different emotional tones. Perhaps the phrase "Oh no." First, they could say it as if they are responding in the negative to a question about whether they are going to the park to play or to a school basketball game. Next, they might use the phrase after discovering that they lost something important to them, like their favorite toy or smartphone. Now have them say "Oh no" reacting to getting caught doing something they shouldn't have like eating too much candy or coming home after their curfew. You can expand on the multiple ways to say the same words with different prosody. Have students alter the stress, rhythm, pitch, and timing in their responses. Tell them they are changing the emotional meaning each time they change their prosody.

Empathy

If you still need convincing that prosody in speech is an important conveyance of emotion, just say "Alexa" or "Hey Google"— "Tell me you love me." They will respond "I love you." But despite years of work to make a computer voice sound human, programmers have been unable to imbue it with emotion. The virtual assistant may say she loves you, but it doesn't sound like she means it.

What all this means for your teaching is that listening to the human voice opens an emotional connection between your students and the speaker, whether the speaker is live in the classroom or being played over speakers or in headphones. Listening to the emotional tone of voice does something very important for your students as listeners. It builds empathy.

Listening triggers empathy because the voice of the person or their story may remind you of someone you know, or it may make you realize they are human, just like you. Hearing triggers an emotional connection. And when you are listening together, as in class, that emotion can bring you together. Emotion connects us to our community and helps us feel like we belong.

The belongingness theory states that people listen to "emotional information (as in oral stories) out of a desire to experience a social connection." Listening decreases our social anxiety and increases our psychological safety, according to research done at the Hebrew University.[28]

In their study, researchers paired up students as speakers and listeners. In one group, the speakers were prompted to tell meaningful stories, such as, "Tell me about a time in your life when you lost someone close to you." In the second group, the speakers told the listeners about a descriptive narrative event, such as, "Tell me about your morning routine." Researchers found that speakers influence the quality of listening because, when they share a meaningful story, they more effectively engage listeners. And when someone is engaged in a story, it's positively associated with psychological safety and negatively associated with social anxiety.

This means that just by presenting your students with good stories with engaging narratives, you can help them improve their listening and their empathy. Listening can help students build social awareness, a core competency in the Collaborative for Academic, Social and Emotional Learning (CASEL)'s framework for social and emotional learning.[29]

But that's not all. A Princeton researcher found that when someone is telling a story, the activity in the brains of his or her listeners begin to match up. Neuroscientist Uri Hasson studies how our brains couple together with sound.[30] He believes communication, speaking, and listening, is "a single act performed by two brains." Hasson used functional magnetic resonance imaging (fMRI) machines to scan the brains of people as they watched a mystery TV show. Then he asked them to retell the story of that show to people who hadn't seen it. As the listeners lay in the fMRI machine, they constructed the story in their minds. And their brain waves looked remarkably similar to the person telling the story. Hasson calls this "neural entrainment"—similar brain waves are produced across listeners.

> *I like that when listening to the stories you can just close your eyes and you can just imagine in your head what is happening.*
> —Fifth-grade student in Elk Grove, CA

Wouldn't you like your class to be in sync like that? Was there ever a time when you looked at your students and saw that they were locked into what you were saying or what you were doing? These experiments prove that it's not happening by accident. Brain coupling is a real phenomenon that you can control by delivering good stories.

This is powerful research. I didn't understand this power as a reporter, but I knew that I could make a connection with listeners by telling a good story. I also intuitively knew that by sharing stories with emotion, I could help listeners empathize.

All this research means listening to stories is a powerful way not only to communicate, but also to bring a group of disparate individuals closer together, increase their sense of well-being, and improve their information retention. And this makes listening a very powerful tool for teaching. But at the heart of it, listening is connecting two human beings. Hearing is the first sense we have as humans and it is one of the last senses to leave us before we die. Hospice workers will tell you it's important to speak to loved ones even when they appear otherwise to not "be there." You are told to play music your loved one enjoys, reminisce about old trips or family gatherings, or read a poem, story, or religious text.

On the final night of my father's life, my relationship with him as his front seat storyteller came full circle. As a child, I used to sit on the front bench seat between my mother and father on long car trips so that I could read the newspaper out loud to my dad.

Forty years later, I sat beside my father again and read him stories at his bedside as he was dying of cancer. I was the only one beside him on the last night of his life, reading to him. My sisters and brother were sleeping in the other rooms, and it was my rotation to spend the night in his room. It's difficult for me to think back to this night, because it scared me to be with him as he struggled to breathe. But he was still conscious enough to tell me to read from a book he recently got for Christmas, *Schulz and Peanuts: A Biography*. My dad loved cartoons, and none more fervently than *Peanuts*.

I stayed up most of the night reading about Schulz's life as my dad slipped in and out of consciousness. At one point, I fell asleep with the book on my lap. When I woke up in the morning, I could see it would be my dad's final day. For the rest of the day, all his children gathered around him quietly talking, telling stories, remembering good times. And we each took a private moment to tell our dad the things we might not have said before. We knew he was listening, and sharing one last story before he died was a powerful moment.

REFLECTION AND PLANNING

Take this opportunity to write some reflections and plans for action.

Make a sound map of your classroom to learn what your classroom sounds like. Note down the sounds students hear in different parts of the room, and at different elevations—sitting on the floor, standing in a corner, maybe even carefully standing on a chair.

Find a story that you connect with emotionally on Listenwise and share it with your students to engage and discuss how the story makes them feel.

How will you practice prosody in your classroom?

Audio Resources

[1] Young, Robin. (2011, April 5). Rescue monkey becomes helping hand after man's accident. *Here & Now*, WBUR, www.wbur.org/hereandnow/2011/04/05/monkey-kasey-ned.

[2] Doucleff, Michaeleen, and Jane Greenhalgh. (2017, February 14). Why killer viruses are on the rise. NPR, www.npr.org/sections/goatsandsoda/2017/02/14/511227050/why-killer-viruses-are-on-the-rise.

[3] Aizenman, Nurith. (2016, October 27). Traveling exhibit shows what it's like to be a refugee. NPR, www.npr.org/2016/10/27/499554303/traveling-exhibit-shows-what-its-like-to-be-a-refugee.

[4] Leipzig, Sam. (2011, November). The Little Rock Nine. PRX, *This Just In*, beta.prx.org/stories/59273-the-little-rock-nine.

References

1. Horowitz, S.S. (2013). In the beginning was the boom. In *The universal sense: How hearing shapes the mind* (pp. 3–5). New York, NY: Bloomsbury.

2. Christensen, C.B., Lauridsen, H., Christensen-Dalsgaard, J., Pedersen, M., & Madsen, P.T. (2015). Better than fish on land? Hearing across metamorphosis in salamanders. *Proceedings of the Royal Society B: Biological Sciences.* *282* (1802): 20141943. doi:10.1098/rspb.2014.1943.

3. NIH. (2020, June 17). *How do we hear?* https://www.nidcd. nih.gov/health/how-do-we-hear (accessed September 16, 2020).

4. Journey of Sound to the Brain (Video). (2020, December 14). National Institute of Deafness and Other Communication Disorders, U.S. Department of Health and Human Services, www.nidcd.nih.gov/health/journey-of-sound-video.

5. Horowitz, S.S. (2013). In the beginning was the boom. In *The universal sense: How hearing shapes the mind* (p. 69). New York, NY: Bloomsbury.

6. Partanen, E., Kujala, T., Näätänen, R., Liitola, A., Sambeth, A., & Huotilainen, M. (2013). Learning-induced neural plasticity of speech processing before birth. *Proceedings of the National Academy of Sciences of the United States of America, 110*(37), 15145–15150. doi:https://doi .org/10.1073/pnas.1302159110.

7. NIH. (2020, June 17). *How do we hear?* https://www.nidcd. nih.gov/health/how-do-we-hear (accessed September 16, 2020).

8. Bergen, B.K. (2012). The polar bear's nose. In *Louder than words: The new science of how the mind makes meaning* (pp. 13–17). New York, NY: Basic Books.

9. Ibid.

10. Aubert, M., Lebe, R., Oktaviana, A.A. et al. (2019). Earliest hunting scene in prehistoric art. *Nature* 576, 442–445. https://doi.org/10.1038/s41586-019-1806-y.

11. Hewlett, B.S., and Roulette, C.J. (2016, January 1). Teaching in hunter–gatherer infancy. *Royal Society Open Science*. royalsocietypublishing.org/doi/10.1098/rsos.150403.

12. Scalise Sugiyama M. (2017). Oral storytelling as evidence of pedagogy in forager societies. *Frontiers in Psychology, 8*, 471. https://doi.org/10.3389/fpsyg.2017.00471.

13. Zak, P.J. (2015). Why inspiring stories make us react: The neuroscience of narrative. *Cerebrum: The Dana Forum on Brain Science, 2015*, 2.

14. Broca-Wernicke Area Small. (n.d.). Wikimedia Commons, Wikimedia, httpps://commons.wikimedia.org/wiki/File:Broca-Wernicke_Area_Small_-_he.png (accessed February 1, 2021).

15. Harte, E. (2020, August 18). How your brain processes language. *Brain World*. https://brainworldmagazine.com/how-your-brain-processes-language/ (accessed September 16, 2020).

16. Foer, J. (2012). *Moonwalking with Einstein: The art and science of remembering everything*. New York, NY: Penguin Press.

17. Recht, D.R., & Leslie, L. (1988). Effect of prior knowledge on good and poor readers' memory of text. *Journal of Educational Psychology, 80*(1), 16–20. https://doi.org/10.1037/0022-0663.80.1.16.

18. Zwaan, R.A. (2003). The immersed experiencer: Toward an embodied theory of language comprehension. *Psychology of Learning and Motivation*, pp. 35–62. doi:10.1016/s0079-7421(03)44002-4.

19. Bergen, B.K. (2012). Keep your mind on the ball. In *Louder than words: The new science of how the mind makes meaning* (pp. 66–69). New York, NY: Basic Books.

20. Zwaan, R., Madden, C., Yaxley, R., & Aveyard, M. (2004). Moving words: Dynamic representations in language comprehension. *Cognitive Science, 28*, 611–619. doi:10.1016/j.cogsci.2004.03.004.

21. Bergen, B.K. (2012). Keep your mind on the ball. In *Louder than words: The new science of how the mind makes meaning* (p. 69). New York, NY: Basic Books.

22. Varao, S., Carriere, J., & Smilek, D. (2013, November 10). *The way we encounter reading material influences how frequently we mind wander.* https://www.frontiersin.org/articles/10.3389/fpsyg.2013.00892/full (accessed September 17, 2020).

23. Wen, T. (2015, July 22). This is your brain on podcasts: Why audio storytelling is so addictive. *The Atlantic*, Atlantic Media Company, www.theatlantic.com/entertainment/archive/2015/04/podcast-brain-why-do-audio-stories-captivate/389925/.

24. Rodero, E. (2012). Stimulating the imagination in a radio story: The role of presentation structure and the degree of involvement of the listener. *Journal of Radio & Audio Media, 19*(1), 45–60. doi:10.1080/19376529.2012.667022.

25. Horowitz, S.S. (2013). In the beginning was the boom. In *The universal sense: How hearing shapes the mind* (p. 126). New York, NY: Bloomsbury.

26. Aeschlimann, M., Knebel, J., Murray, M.M., & Clarke, S. (2008). Emotional pre-eminence of human vocalizations. *Brain Topography, 20*(4), 239–248. doi:10.1007/s10548-008-0051-8.

27. Common Sense Media. (2018). *The common sense census: Media use by tweens and teens* (pp. 1–104, Rep.). New York, NY: Common Sense Media.

28. Itzchakov, G., Castro, R.D., & Kluger, A.N. (2014, March). *If you want people to listen to you, tell a story.* A presentation given at the 35th annual International Listening Association convention, Minneapolis, MN.

29. SEL: What are the core competence areas and where are they promoted? CASEL, casel.org/sel-framework/.

30. Hasson, U., Ghazanfar, A.A., Galantucci, B., Garrod, S., & Keysers, C. (2012). Brain-to-brain coupling: A mechanism for creating and sharing a social world. *Trends in Cognitive Sciences, 16*(2), 114–121. doi:10.1016/j.tics.2011.12.007.

Chapter **4**

How to Teach Listening

"It's time to take out your journals," Vicki calls above the din of 25 students chattering.

"Class! You are not listening to me!" she repeats even louder.

As her frustration level builds, Vicki finds herself repeating over and over, "Kids—listen to me!"

But then it dawns on her. Has she taught them how to listen?

Not just how to listen to her instructions, but to all the content she's delivering every day. She stands at the front of the class telling her students so many important things every day—reviewing fractions, detailing the life cycle of water, reading aloud from "Locomotion"—but are they really listening? Has she done enough to teach them how to listen?

Vicki thinks for a moment about all the classroom instruction time spent on improving their writing and math skills and understanding historical events and scientific concepts. She's consulted blogs and books on how to improve reading. She would never dream of telling her students to "Just read!" without first teaching them the building blocks of reading.

But she is often telling her students "Just listen!"

She decides it's time for some reflection on how to teach the listening skills she wants her students to be using. But where to start?

BUILD AWARENESS

Teaching listening is easier than you might think. With some simple steps to build awareness, learn strategies, and apply what they've learned, your students will become better listeners.

I haven't found a study that quantifies how much class time is wasted by teachers repeating themselves because students aren't listening. But it's safe to say that teachers explain ideas several times, repeat instructions, and admonish their students to pay attention and listen. The consequences of not listening can include students missing important concepts or instructional time needed to master critical skills. There is a cascade effect caused by not listening well the first time.

As with any skill set, students vary in the listening skills they bring to the classroom. That's why it's best to start with building self-awareness. The concept that listening is a skill that can be learned and practiced may be new to them. Undoubtedly, they have been criticized many times in their lives for not listening. It begins with their caregivers or parents. They are the first adults who are casualties in the listening battle. The fight continues when kids go to preschool and it's the first time they are part of a larger group with a need to listen to group instructions. If they don't hear their teacher say "It's time to put away the blocks," they could face consequences.

As the battle moves to elementary school, the importance of listening to learn continues to grow. Now listening is not just something they need to do well to transition between activities or to learn how to tie their shoes. They need to listen to learn about academic concepts such as multiplication, character traits in folktales, animal adaptations, or geographical features.

And yet, when are students learning how to listen?

Studies link listening skills to literacy and academic success but listening instruction in the K–12 classroom is practically nonexistent.[1] The lack of effective listening programs is premised on the fact that there is a dearth of research on effective listening strategies in primary and secondary schools. And researchers haven't spent time in K–12 classrooms to identify effective listening strategies. Much of the listening research focuses on how listening plays into learning to speak another language.

When I started Listenwise in 2014, I honestly didn't think I was starting a listening skills-building company that would break new ground by helping students become more effective listeners. I had been a public radio reporter for 20 years and believed Listenwise would help students learn from the real-world news stories and podcasts. I saw how topics, books, and concepts taught in K–12 classrooms were covered in the news. Curating these stories for teachers, I believed, would be a powerful way to engage students. And, I thought, listening is an easy way to do it. Everyone can listen.

At that time, I did not know that listening comprehension as a skill was not often purposefully taught in schools and that children typically had very little exposure to authentic audio resources in their learning. It was generally assumed that because students come to kindergarten hearing, they can listen, and that school instruction should focus on teaching them how to read, write, and calculate.

After launching the first version of the Listenwise website with a collection of a few hundred audio stories with listening comprehension and discussion questions, we received our first request from teachers to help them teach listening skills better. That's when I realized that Listenwise had a bigger mission than bringing authentic audio stories to students, it needed to help teachers learn how to teach listening.

The good news is that listening skills can be taught, and it can be done in ways that are engaging and fun and address curriculum standards. Teaching foundational listening skills builds important learning skills.

Class Activity: Building Your Listening Profile

Helping your students identify their own behaviors and some of their own ideas about how they can correct their bad listening habits is a great way to start improving their listening. Just being aware can change behavior. Use your judgment to guide students in their reflection.

Elementary School Students: Start by describing *hearing* as when someone can physically perceive a sound with their senses. You might share that a deaf person may have little to no hearing. Ask students to close their eyes and then clap your hands. Tell students to give a silent thumbs up if they heard a sound. Next, tell students *listening* is when someone gives their complete attention to a sound in order to understand it. Ask students to explain what caused the sound they just heard even though their eyes were closed. Share that explaining the sound they heard is one way to show they gave their attention to the sound and understood what caused it.

Ask students to listen to and identify all the sounds of the room in which they're sitting. Can they hear a heater or air conditioner? Breathing of classmates? Chairs moving? Feet or pencils tapping? Someone walking by in the hall? Ask students if they can describe for the class the sounds they heard.

If they are learning from home, students can still do this exercise and share on Zoom or by a written response or drawing a sketch of what they heard.

Share with students the S.L.A.N.T. strategy popularized by Doug Lemov in *Teach Like a Champion*.[2] This tool can help them remember what behaviors they can use to be better active listeners. The letters stand for: Sit up. Lean toward the speaker. Ask questions. Nod your head. Track the speaker with your eyes. Ask students to S.L.A.N.T. as you read aloud a fictional conversation between two students. You could also ask a student in class to role play the scenario with you.

Student 1: I'm so scared.

Student 2: What's wrong?

Student 1: My family is taking a trip, and we're flying. I've never flown, and I'm scared something might happen.

Student 2: I love flying. I flew to Disneyland once. It was the best trip. We stayed for a week. Are you excited? When do you leave? Where are you going?

Ask the class to identify what Student 1 was focused on. (They were worried about flying.) Ask the class if Student 2 acted like they cared about what Student 1 said. (No, they disregarded their concerns.) Did Student 2 respond? (Yes.) If so, did the response seem focused on Student 1 or focused on themselves? (They focused on themselves.) What is Student 2 ignoring the concern of Student 1 evidence of? (They judged what was said as unimportant.)

Tell students that when they listen to anything, they should S.L.A.N.T. as well as listen to understand and not just respond. Share that when we begin thinking about our own response we stop actively listening.

Middle/High School Students: Ask students to think about behaviors they believe keep them from being good listeners. They should write them down. Ask students to share one thing they wrote down and see whether other students have similar behaviors. Now ask students to build a list of what they believe to be good listening skills. Again, ask students to share one thing they wrote down and see whether other students have similar ideas. Have students make individual listening profiles that identify their strengths and weaknesses as a listener.

It's important to recognize that there are many different types of listening. We listen all the time for a variety of purposes whether we know it or not. In fact, our hearing sense is never turned off, even when we are sleeping. We are aware of sounds that might wake us in the middle of the night in a heightened sense of alert. If someone calls your name across a crowded noisy room, you are likely to hear it. You can't turn off your listening.

Helping students understand this about their hearing and listening will help them understand that they need to focus their listening to get the most out of instruction, a conversation, or other opportunities for auditory learning. In school you will likely be focusing on building students' precise, strategic, and critical listening skills. You should explain to your students that focus and help them understand why these types of listening will help them become better learners.

TYPES OF LISTENING

There are several different types of listening. I drew on others' work to determine which ones I believe are the most important to recognize and use in the classroom.[3] I'll focus on five types here and discuss which types you may want to focus on with your students. But overall, it helps to walk through these different types of listening with your students so they understand how much they are already working their listening muscles.

Discriminative Listening

This type of listening is about distinguishing sounds. Is that a bird calling or the microwave beeping? Should I be concerned about a sound or let it pass by unnoticed? All hearing humans practice this type of listening more than any other. We are born with it. Discriminative listening also allows us to know how many people are talking, whether the pitch of a voice is high or low, and if they sound old or young. We are also intuitively listening to the tone, pace, and emotion in what we hear. We are processing all this input at the same rate as we are hearing it and not even thinking about the skills required of our brain to do discriminative listening.

Class Practice
Elementary School Students: Tell the class you are going to take them on a virtual trip someplace within the United States using the Acoustic Atlas. [1] Ask students to make three columns on a piece of paper headed What I hear, What I visualize and Where this is. Select sounds from the Acoustic Atlas and play them one at a time, providing time for students to jot down notes. Ask students

to share their observations and inferences before showing photos of the sound sources from the Acoustic Atlas.

Next, take the class outside and ask them to listen and notice one or two sounds they can share with their classmates. When back in the classroom, ask them to share what sounds they noticed and what was making each sound.

Middle/High School Students: Ask the class to be completely silent for two minutes. While silent, they should be listening to all the sounds going on inside and outside the classroom that they might not otherwise notice. Ask students to take a few notes on what they hear. Is there a fan making noise? Is there another class walking by the room? Identify sounds that typically would go unnoticed to teach your students that they are always discriminatively listening because they don't pay attention to these sounds on a regular basis.

Precise Listening

You use this type of listening if you've ever asked for directions. You are listening for a precise set of details. You need to be able to remember these details, often in the sequence you heard them. Often, this type of listening comes after you ask a question, so you are ready to listen for the answer. Students need to listen precisely to their teachers' instructions on a regular basis.

Class Practice

Elementary School Students: Play "I spy" as a class, asking one student to select an object in the classroom that all can see. The student gives verbal clues saying, "I spy with my little eye something that. . ." Clues could indicate color, size, shape, location, texture, or function. Remind students that they are listening to details and using their precise listening skills.

Middle/High School Students: Ask a student to describe how to walk from the classroom to the library or the cafeteria. Have them use as many details as possible. Using precise language will improve the other students' precise listening skills. You may need to prompt the student to add detail. When you turn left, what is hanging on the wall? About how many steps from the doorway to the library? Then ask one or two other students to retell the sequence of the answer. How well did they use their precise listening skills? What did they leave out and would that be an important factor in understanding?

Strategic Listening

Listening for comprehension of substantive material, from a lecture to a radio broadcast, is the listening skill most often used in learning. It allows the listener to identify the main idea, summarize what was said, and make inferences from what they heard. We all practice this type of listening on a regular basis. Students are using this type of listening skill in school probably more than any other as they absorb so much content during the day. They are trying to understand and make sense of the messages they hear. When strategically listening, learners should understand the importance of getting the main idea to be able to summarize what they heard.

Class Practice

Elementary School Students: Any story has characters, conflicts, and resolutions. Select a 30-second Weird News story on Listenwise (a free account gives you access). Tell students they will practice strategic listening using a short, high interest story. Ask students to make five columns on a piece of paper labeled Somebody, Wanted, But, So, and Then. This exercise is adapted from Kylene Beers' SWBS approach to summarize a reading.[4] Explain the following: "Somebody" refers to one character in the story. "Wanted" refers to what a character wanted to do or wanted to obtain. "But" refers to a challenge or problem a character faced. "So" refers to what a character did to address the challenge. "Then" refers to the effect of a choice a character made.

First, play the story once for the gist. Next, play the story a second time asking students to identify any words or phrases they did not understand. Finally, play the story a third time asking students to use their graphic organizers to listen for who the characters were, what they wanted, challenges they faced, how they responded, and what happened in the end. Ask students to share their observations with partners. Then ask partners to share with the whole class what their partners observed.

Middle/High School Students: Strategic listening can be practiced in multiple ways in your classroom. You could select any story on Listenwise or from a public radio station and ask students to identify the main idea. Listenwise has hundreds of multiple-choice quizzes that test students on their strategic listening skills by asking them to identify the main idea and make an inference, among other skills. You could also do an activity following a school assembly with a guest speaker or, after reading a chapter of a book aloud, ask students to summarize the chapter and think about how it relates to the rest of the story.

Critical Listening

When you are listening critically you are evaluating the speaker's point of view or working to analyze what's being said. You are looking for clues from the speaker to discern what's relevant and what's supported by evidence. Critical listening requires listening to and carefully evaluating a message before forming and sharing an opinion or responding with a fact. This can be the hardest type of listening because it requires you to be actively listening for a specific purpose and using higher order critical thinking skills.

Class Practice

Elementary School Students: To practice this, give students a series of open-ended questions that will elicit different responses. You might consider mixing questions that can be answered based on opinions with questions that might be answered based on facts related to what you're studying in class. Ask students to make three columns on a piece of paper labeled: Review, Reflect, and Respond.

Explain the following: When students "review" what they hear, they consider (1) what surprised them, (2) what challenged what they believe, (3) what changed how they think, (4) what confirmed what they already knew.

When students "reflect," they consider how they feel based on what they heard. Do they feel calm or angry? Do they agree or disagree? Do they feel confident or confused?

Tell students that when they respond, they should consider if they're responding to an *opinion* or a *fact*. Remind the class that differences in opinions are common, deserve to be recognized, and may elicit different emotional responses in each of us. Share that differences regarding facts can be settled by turning to a credible source of information to help guide a discussion.

Middle/High School Students: One way to practice critical listening is conducting a debate. If you search "debate" on Listenwise you will find dozens of stories that set up two sides of an issue for your class to debate. Instruct students to choose a position on the debate topic and listen critically for the facts and relevant points that support their position in the story. You could also ask them to judge the relative strength of each viewpoint presented in the story.

Appreciative Listening

We all enjoy appreciative listening. We do it when listening to music, going to the theater, or watching a movie. It's simple, joyful, and not too hard on the brain. It's good to discuss what elements of a song or movie make for the most satisfying appreciative listening.

Class Practice

Elementary School Students: Remind students that appreciative listening is about taking in sounds for our own personal enjoyment. Share with students the website A Soft Murmur. [2] Show students how they can play and adjust the volume of individual sounds and create their own unique mix of sounds. Encourage students to create their own unique mix of sounds and share them with others in the class. Ask them to explain why they chose the sounds for each mix and any volume adjustments they made.

Middle/High School Students: Ask students what their favorite sound is. You might share your favorite sound first. Maybe it's the crashing waves of the ocean or a heavy rain storm. Then discuss why they appreciate this sound. What about it gives them pleasure? What memories does the sound evoke? Tell them that when using their appreciative listening skills, they connect with their emotions.

Educator Story: Teaching Critical Thinking with Listening

Listening is a skill set, not a content area belonging to one discipline. California, where I teach the Common Core, lists six standards related to speaking and listening in grades K–12. For listening, emphasis is placed on summarizing key points, identifying claims made by a speaker, and pinpointing reasons and evidence used to support claims.

I start by selecting a short, engaging audio story to play for my students. This year I used the NPR story "Repentant Thief Regrets Swiping Heinz Ketchup." [3] On Listenwise it's called "The Ketchup Thief." It is a 26-second-long story that has characters, a problem, a solution, and a twist ending.

I shared with students we would listen to a 26-second story one time for the gist. I asked them if that sounded like a long or short. All agreed it sounded short compared to stories they've been asked to read in the past.

After the first listen, I asked students to share what stood out to them. A handful offered one or two points. The rest of the class was silent. I asked students to think for a moment about their thinking. Did they know what to listen for? Did a 26-second story have too much information to process all at once? Students agreed they liked the story, but were struggling to identify what was most important.

I said we would listen to the same story a second time and use a graphic organizer to help focus on key points. The tool we used was a chart created by Kylene Beers with columns labeled: "Somebody wanted, But, So, Then."

I explained they should listen for any characters who were trying to get something (Somebody wanted). Next, they should listen for any challenges the characters faced as they were on their quest (But). How did the characters react? What did they do? Their choices would be the effect in response to the challenge they faced (So). Finally, what was the result of the actions the characters took (Then)?

As students listened a second time, they knew what to listen for. They paused, backed up, relistened to parts, and discussed with other classmates what they thought. The transformation was instantaneous. Students had a purpose for listening and a chance to actively interrogate a piece of audio rather than passively listen to it.

When we discussed the story a second time as a whole class, students were ready to talk about characters, the challenges they faced, the causes and effects that transpired, and they were also prepared to make inferences based on what they heard. By using a tool like "Somebody wanted, But, So, Then" to interrogate a piece of audio, I was able to teach students how to approach listening as compared to teaching them what an individual audio story said. To promote lifelong learners and critical thinkers, we have to explicitly teach students how to listen using carefully selected tools and strategies.

—Jim Bentley, fifth-grade teacher,
Elk Grove, CA

MODELING GOOD LISTENING

Everyone loves listening to a good story. You can see listeners perk up their ears, lean in, and want to hear a compelling narrative. Good stories, told aloud, have the power to captivate even the most reluctant readers. While storytelling is important, "scholars are beginning to emphasize the need to refocus on story listening."[5] This is especially true in live storytelling situations where the narrator responds to good listeners and the listeners affect the narrators.

The listening instruction we've built into the Listenwise platform is based on research that shows everyone loves listening to a good story, and that better stories make better listeners.

A study at Hebrew University found evidence that the quality of the oral story affected the quality of the listening. In other words, "the narrative determines the listening."[6] In another study of story listeners, researchers found that visualization is central to the process of listening to stories. "Visualize what is happening" was the top-ranked strategy of good listeners.[7]

> *I recognize how much listening improves students' visualization skills because the sounds of the story are authentic. The sounds provide rich descriptive material for students to imagine and bring them closer to the facts and knowledge.*
> —Kara Nierman, seventh-grade teacher, Woonsocket, RI

As a teacher, you are the center of attention for the school day. How you deliver information and how you model good listening will have a big impact on your students. They are listening to you all the time, maybe not always actively and attentively, but they are listening. Engaging them with stories and giving them a sense of emotional safety can help to improve their skills.

But this doesn't have to rest entirely on your shoulders. There are hundreds of engaging audio stories from episodic podcasts, audio books, and your local public radio station. Listenwise is the only instructional resource with thousands of narrative nonfiction audio stories curated for classroom use. The lessons are aligned to curriculum standards and include listening for comprehension questions that can help students build their precise, strategic, and critical listening skills.

The audio stories found on public radio or in podcasts are often filled with authentic, actual events and diverse perspectives on the world. This makes them inherently engaging to students. If we apply what we've learned from the Hebrew University study mentioned earlier, then we want to embrace teaching with descriptive narratives. Listing key facts and dates relevant to the start of World War I isn't the same as listening to the NPR story "A Century Ago in Sarajevo: a Plot, a Farce and a Fateful Shot."[4] The story transports students to the street corner where the assassination happened in 1914. The reporter is there in the present day and sets up the story as a "tale." He explains how the street corner where Archduke Franz Ferdinand was shot looks today and what it would have looked like more than a hundred years ago. The narrator/reporter says the events of the day are hard to overstate because it started a global war that killed millions of people. If you listen to the story, which is about 5 minutes long, you learn that the assassins never intended to start a global war. By the end of the story it certainly leaves you wanting to know more. It's a perfect start to a unit on World War I.

APPLYING LISTENING PRACTICE

Applying Bloom's taxonomy to listening instruction is an excellent place to start. Bloom's taxonomy was developed in the 1950s to promote higher forms of thinking in education.[8]

The taxonomy has been revised and updated by others over the years. After each listening exercise, ask students a series of questions that build thinking skills along Bloom's taxonomy. Can they remember a detail from the story? Do they understand the main idea? How could what they heard in the story apply to something else they know?

On the Listenwise platform there is a bank of four to six listening comprehension questions at various levels of Bloom's taxonomy connected to every podcast. Listenwise also provides listening discussion questions about each story that engage students in higher order thinking skills. These questions ask students to analyze, synthesize, or evaluate ideas in the stories and apply those ideas to their own experiences.

Class Activity: Evaluating Listening Comprehension

Using questions that vary in cognitive demand is an excellent way to evaluate the listener's comprehension level as well as their ability to apply what they've heard. Here is an example of a set of questions from the NPR story previously mentioned in this chapter about the start of World War I.

Listening Comprehension Questions

What factors contributed to the archduke's assassination, according to the story?

What chain of events led to the assassination of Archduke Ferdinand?

What does the historian mean when he says that the assassination "seems almost farcical"?

Who were the people intending to assassinate the archduke, according to the story?

Discussion Themes

What does this story suggest about how the choices people make can direct the course of history? Support your answer with details from the story.

If you could go back in time and change one event in history, what would it be?

The audio for this story and a full lesson called "The Shot That Started World War I" can be found at https://listenwise.com/book.

Breaking down the activities before, during, and after listening can also support effective listening instruction. I go into more depth around this strategy later in the chapter.

You might assume that listening fits best in the language arts curriculum because of its relationship to reading and developmental language skills. You might also think that listening skills should only be taught in primary grades, when students are more open to oral storytelling.

Don't limit your listening instruction! Children of all ages and grades can and should learn to be effective listeners and continue to develop and apply their skills.

Mary Jalongo, author of *Learning to Listen, Listening to Learn*, defines an effective listener as someone who takes in the message accurately and interprets it appropriately no matter the context.[9] Jalongo says that integrating listening activities throughout the day and across the curriculum is the best approach to developing effective listeners. Just as we are all listening and learning throughout our days, so should students. Jalongo recognizes that listening is sometimes harder than reading because you have to listen at the pace of the speaker, you can't preview what's going to be said or look back to review, and you often don't have the transcript to read along.

If you are a middle school science teacher opening a unit on acids and bases, you might start with an engaging story that explains the real-world effects of what happens when bases turn acidic. The story "Acidic Oceans Dissolving Shellfish Industry" takes students out on the ocean to an oyster boat with a fisherman. [5] The story is about farming shellfish and how ocean acidification is hurting the ability of oysters to grow seed, or baby oysters. By listening to this story at the start of a unit, students understand how the subject relates to them and the food they eat. They are hearing the voices and perspectives of fishermen, scientists, and businesspeople involved in the shell-fishing industry. They gain important background knowledge about the fishing industry and how it's being impacted by climate change.

Guidelines for Teaching Listening

Before Listening

Set a Goal

It's important to have a goal or purpose for every listening activity. Stating a purpose will give students guidance to know where to focus, enabling them to achieve success.[10]

Build Background

Help students connect what they already know with what they will hear in the audio story by asking questions about their personal experiences with the topic. Explain what students need to understand before listening, preview vocabulary words, invite them to think about relevant prior knowledge, anticipate the subject of the story, or otherwise engage actively in preparing for the story.

Prepare the Environment

If playing the story out loud to the whole class, minimize distraction by making the environment at home or in school as quiet as possible. Use headphones for listening when possible.

Introduce Listening Strategies

Introduce tools and strategies for successful listening (see below).

During Listening

Note-Taking Strategies

Students can use a listening organizer to help them focus on important ideas and details while listening to the story, which can help to deepen their understanding. Listening organizers might include T-charts, Venn diagrams, or a blank page to keep track of a character's actions in the story. Such organizers can guide students in taking notes to help them focus their listening and teach them strategies to support comprehension in other contexts.

Problem-Solving Strategies

If students do not understand a word or concept, they can use clues from the story to make a guess. If they are listening independently, they can stop the audio and think or listen again as needed to ensure understanding. They can be "problem-solving listeners." These strategies should be taught before students begin listening, with reminders provided as needed.

After Listening

Reflect on the Audio Story

Engage students in synthesizing what they learned from listening to the story with a focus on key understanding goals. For example, ask students to respond to listening comprehension questions in writing and then share their responses with a partner, small group, or the whole class. Discuss key themes in the story and encourage students to make connections to other texts or experiences. Students can respond to questions about the story through writing, speaking in conversation, recording themselves speaking, or a combination.

While listening and reading both require comprehension skills, many of which overlap, the application of those skills can vary somewhat across contexts. For example, students need to practice identifying and summarizing the most important ideas in audio stories, which can be organized differently than print stories. And practicing identifying the main idea of a podcast will help students find the main idea in reading as well.

The type of natural speech found in these audio stories typically does not follow the structure of a written article with a clearly articulated lead and a linear progression of ideas. When students are listening to a speaker's voice, they can also pay attention to the tone, emphasis, and pacing of the speech to make inferences and identify the speaker's point of view.

We recommend assessing listening comprehension in one of two ways—using the formative multiple choice auto-scored online listening quizzes on Listenwise or the listening comprehension questions, which can be answered online, handwritten, or discussed in class. If you administer the quizzes, you can track a learner's skills and progress on a dashboard. As the measurements for listening have improved, we have begun to focus more on three core components of listening: identifying the main idea, recognizing literal meaning, and making inferences. I go into more detail about assessing listening in a later chapter.

Class Activity: Using Clues to Make an Inference

Elementary School Students: Your students can practice making inferences with the Earth Rangers episode "Wild Wetlands and Mighty Metamorphosizing Frogs." [6] The story follows Earth Ranger Emma as she goes on the hunt for frogs. It incorporates sounds of bugs and walking through the mud. By listening to the story, can students infer the location of the story using the audio clues?

What can students infer by listening to these sentences in the story:

"Frogs go through metamorphosis for a couple of reasons. One of the main ones is that it's important for them to have different life stages to spread out the competition so that the juveniles don't compete with the adults and the adults don't eat or compete with the juveniles."

Why are frogs vulnerable during metamorphosis?

What are the advantages of staying tadpoles for years and years?

Middle/High School Students: Use the NPR story "The Sound of Laughter Can Be Key in Determining People's Relationships." [7] Listen to the story then present the following quotation from the story:

"Laughter is a social experience. So if you're living alone right now, watching a funny movie is not going to get you to laugh necessarily. So maybe try doing, like, a Netflix party or something where you could laugh with other people because it's really good for you."

The inference that students should make is that people are more likely to laugh at something funny with other people around.

The audio in both of these stories can also be found at https://listenwise.com/book.

THE MENTAL PROCESS OF LISTENING: METACOGNITIVE SKILLS

Today, many students' listening skills are first tested when they learn a second language. It's uncommon for them to be aware of, or tested on, their listening comprehension in their first language.

It's widely understood that you cannot learn to speak another language without intensively listening to it. The "listening lab" in a language class is one of the common ways students practice listening. Listening helps you understand the meaning of words in context. It allows you to hear words spoken that you may previously have only seen written. Listening is probably the best practice for understanding a language that is new to you.

The research around developing good listening skills is almost entirely focused on developing listening comprehension in second language scenarios. Very little research has been conducted on improving listening in your first language.

> *Focusing on listening skills is unique in our visual world. It is very challenging to develop listening skills.*
> —Lisa Goldman, seventh-grade Social Studies teacher, Walpole, MA

Listening metacognition researchers Laura Janusik and Shaughan Keaton say that research into second language listening strategies and competencies has "thrived" while there aren't comparable measures and strategies in first language listening. They wanted to see if the ways listening is measured in second language scenarios could also apply to first language listening scenarios.[11]

First, it's important to break down the difference between cognitive listening and metacognitive listening. Cognitive listening is the understanding or comprehending part of listening. Janusik explains "as cognitive listening aids in comprehension, then, metacognitive listening assists in monitoring the listening process."

It is important to help your students develop both cognitive and metacognitive listening skills. For instance, after listening to a three-minute story, can your students understand what the story is about and identify the main idea (cognitive)? Can they use the surrounding context to decipher an unfamiliar word (metacognitive)?

It's the metacognitive skills I want to focus on as an avenue to help students become better listeners. You will be helping students understand their mental processes as they listen. They will be thinking about their listening. These self-monitoring strategies are used during listening so that students can be aware of their abilities.

Researcher Janusik and Keaton tested the metacognitive listening strategies they identified in learning a second language to see if they also worked in first language listening scenarios. From their research they developed a new instrument called the Janusik-Keaton Metacognitive Listening Strategies Instrument or MLSI.[12]

MLSI—Metacognitive Listening Strategies Instrument

To make students aware of their metacognitive listening skills, review the three strategies below before listening. Tell students they should be using the metacognitive listening strategies of problem solving, planning and directed attention while listening.

Problem Solving: Students will not know every word or concept they hear. They will need to problem solve. They can guess the meaning of some words and see if it makes sense. Tell them it's okay to make guesses. Tell them to use the overall idea of the story to help their understanding of words or concepts they don't know. They will be "problem-solving listeners."

Planning-Evaluation: You should set a goal for listening. This is not telling your students how to listen, but telling them what ideas, details, or words they should be listening for. As they build their listening muscle, it's important that you help set achievable goals for listening. And after the listening, assess whether they reached that goal. And ask them to reflect and evaluate their own listening.

Directed Attention: Share with your students that it's common for your mind to wander when listening, but they need to direct their attention back to the task. You could use note-taking strategies or graphic organizers to guide their attention. Tell them that listening is a constantly evolving task and if they misunderstand something, they can adjust based on what they hear to correct their own misunderstanding.

(Source: Informed by Janusik and Shaughan's work on Listening Metacognition)

WHERE TO LISTEN

There are challenges to teaching in an ideal listening environment. In most classrooms it might be impossible. Classrooms are noisy, hallway sounds are distracting, and there are often disruptions from the loudspeaker. In a remote setting, you don't have control over your student's home learning environment. It's good to recognize this and discuss the challenges with your students. We are listening all the time, so practicing listening in a variety of different circumstances will help focus students' attention and build their effective listening skills.

But as much as you can control the circumstance, it's important to set up a good listening environment so that when students are practicing the skill, they can be as focused as possible. When you are conducting a dedicated listening activity, you could close the classroom door to avoid distractions and maybe turn down the lights so students don't get distracted by visuals. You might invite students to close their eyes while listening if they are not using a note-taking strategy. If your students are listening to a podcast independently, they can listen at their desks with headphones. Or they can be seated looking at the front of the classroom where you might display the interactive transcript if you are using Listenwise. Otherwise, you might show a picture related to the story they are hearing. Listening works very well in blended or flipped classrooms because it can easily be an individual student experience.

Encouraging your students to listen while doing another activity is also a good way to practice the skill. In fact, we do most of our listening on the go because listening is portable. Many older students have smartphones that can download and store podcasts. That means students can get up and move while listening. You could incorporate content-based stories during gym class. You could assign listening that could be completed while they are walking or taking the bus home.

> *I received close to 100% participation on any Listenwise assignment I give to my students (in remote learning).*
> —Eileen Garza, high school English I and III teacher, Colton, CA

As our world changed in 2020, I noticed something that grew out of the shift to remote teaching during the school shutdowns in the coronavirus pandemic. Teachers and students were listening more. As students were required to do more of their learning online, staring for hours at a computer, teachers gravitated to activities that could be done without watching or typing on a screen. Teachers told me the listening activities they assigned during remote learning had a higher completion rate. When students are "Zoomed out," listening can be a relaxing break for your eyes. And it can provide an emotional connection. At a time when students feel disconnected and isolated from each other, listening to other people's stories, the emotion in their voices, and their perspectives can help them feel a human connection.

REFLECTION AND PLANNING

Take this opportunity to write some reflections and plans for action.

How will you discuss and practice different types of listening with your students?

_____

_____

Choose a subject or topic to start with and consider the materials you need to start. Think about what listening skill you will focus on first. Main idea?

_____

_____

In what ways might you implement the metacognitive strategies around listening?

_____

_____

Look at your scope and sequence and write down a few topics that you will be teaching in the next few weeks that could include a listening exercise.

_____

_____

Audio Resources

[1] Acoustic Atlas: Montana State University MSU Library. _Acoustic Atlas: Montana State University Library_, https://acousticatlas.org/index.php.

[2] A Soft Murmur, https://asoftmurmur.com/.

[3] Repentant thief regrets swiping Heinz ketchup. (2019, August 13). NPR, www.npr.org/2019/08/13/750709284/repentant-thief-regrets-swiping-heinz-ketchup.

[4] Shapiro, Ari. (2014, June 27). A century ago in Sarajevo: A plot, a farce and a fateful shot. NPR, www.npr.org/2014/06/27/325516359/a-century-ago-in-sarajevo-a-plot-a-farce-and-a-fateful-shot.

[5] Dornfeld, A. (2010, April 8). Acidic oceans dissolving shellfish industry. *The Environment Report,* https://environmentreport.org/?tag=acid.

[6] Podcast. (2020, January 10). Episode 6: Earth rangers: Where kids go to save animals! *Earth Rangers,* www.earthrangers.com/wildwire/podcast/episode-6/.

[7] Cornish, Audie, & Kelly, Mary Louise. (2020, October 9). The sound of laughter can be key in determining people's relationships. NPR, www.npr.org/2020/10/09/922375817/the-sound-of-laughter-can-be-key-in-determining-people-s-relationships.

References

1. Brigman, G., Lane, D., Switzer, D., Lane, D., & Lawrence, R. (1999). Teaching children school success skills. *Journal of Educational Research, 92*(6), 323–329. http://www.jstor.org/stable/27542233 (accessed September 13, 2020).

2. Lemov, D. (2010). *Teach like a champion: Grades K–12.* San Francisco, CA: Jossey-Bass.

3. 6 Common types of listening you should know. (2014, August 27). https://medium.com/@Relationship_Up/6-common-types-of-listening-you-should-know-42b088c175dc (accessed September 13, 2020).

4. Beers, K., & G. Kylene Beers. (2003). *When kids can't read, what teachers can do: A guide for teachers, 6–12.* Portsmouth, NH: Heinemann.

5. Cohen, S.D., & Wolvin, A.D. (2011). Listening to stories: An initial assessment of student listening characteristics. *Listening Education, 2,* 17–27.

6. Itzchakov, G., Castro, R.D., & Kluger, A.N. (2014, March). *If you want people to listen to you, tell a story.* A presentation given at the 35th annual International Listening Association convention, Minneapolis, MN.

7. Cohen, S.D., & Wolvin, A.D. (2011). Listening to stories: An initial assessment of student listening characteristics. *Listening Education, 2,* 17–27.

8. Bloom, B.S., Engelhart, M.D., Furst, E.J., Hill, W.H., & Krathwohl, D.R. (1956). *Taxonomy of educational objectives: The classification of educational goals.* London, UK: Longman.

9. Jalongo, M.R. (2008). *Learning to listen, listening to learn: Building essential skills in young children.* Washington, DC: National Association for the Education of Young Children.

10. Funk, H.D., & Funk, G.D. (1989). Guidelines for developing listening skills. *The Reading Teacher, 42,* 198–206.

11. Janusik, L. & Keaton, S. (2011). Listening metacognitions: Another key to teaching listening? *Listening Education 3,* 33–44.

12. Janusik, L. (2017). Metacognitive listening strategies instrument (MLSI). *The Sourcebook of Listening Research,* 438–444. doi:10.1002/9781119102991.ch46.

Chapter 5

The Intersection Between Listening and Reading

Vicki has one student who is still struggling to read. And it's really bothering her. Ayesha is a bright kid with good focus and attention. She is always the first to put up her hand to answer a question after listening to a passage that was read aloud. She typically understands the gist of the books she's reading.

But when Vicki goes around the class asking students to read aloud certain passages, Ayesha really struggles. She omits words, inserts words, and sometimes adds prefixes and suffixes that aren't there.

Vicki referred her to the reading specialist, who tested her for dyslexia. The results weren't conclusive. She told her to slow down her reading. Ayesha is doing well in class, so Vicki is not very concerned. But something is still blocking her from being a fully proficient reader and she can't figure out how to help her.

Vicki remembers when the class listened to a podcast together and read along with the transcript. They then answered listening comprehension questions. Ayesha excelled. She got every question right. Maybe this is the key to helping Ayesha become a better reader—focus on how listening can help with her reading.

BETTER LISTENERS = BETTER READERS

Better listeners make better readers. This is documented by studies that show listening skills have been linked to literacy at an early age.[1] A true picture of a student's literacy lies in understanding both reading and listening skills together, according to research.[2] But not everyone understands how powerful this connection is and what you as a teacher or parent can do about it.

My daughter had similar challenges to Ayesha's.

She was struggling to read at the same rate as her classmates. She could decode smaller words but struggled with more complex phonic challenges such as multisyllabic words. She hopped over words. And she often read words incorrectly. For example, she read the word "like" as "lick." Even as she got older, she sometimes made simple words more complex, such as reading the word "recent" as "reception." She didn't realize it didn't make sense. And often she didn't know she read the word incorrectly.

She was tested for a reading disability. She went to an eye specialist to determine if it was an eye tracking issue. Her reading problems were diagnosed using a process of elimination to determine what they *weren't*. She wasn't a classic dyslexic. She didn't have eye tracking problems. She started to get pull-out reading help. But then I noticed something at home.

As a reporter for NPR, news radio was the backdrop to everything that happened in our kitchen and in our car. For a long time, I didn't even think my two daughters were listening to the news with me. As they grew older, they would sometimes ask questions about a story, surprising me with their deep understanding of a complex topic. But I didn't know how connected listening skills and reading skills were until my younger daughter was in the third grade. She was asking me very sophisticated questions about stories she heard on NPR. She was listening and understanding the high level of academic vocabulary in audio stories.

If I had given my daughter the printed transcript of the radio story, she would not have been able to read it. The sentences and words were too complex. This discovery led me to support her with more audio books and podcasts. Those audio books enabled her to grasp the concepts and content she needed to learn. They engaged her in subjects beyond what she could read on the page. I selected NPR stories for her to listen to that complemented what she was studying in school so she would feel confident going into class to learn.

The realization of the interconnectedness between listening and reading compelled me to start Listenwise, because I could see how listening to podcasts supported her and could help others.

For instance, when my daughter was studying the arrival of the Pilgrims in North America, I found a commentary on NPR by author Nathaniel Philbrick called "Debunking Pilgrim Myths: Before Plymouth." [1] It was a sophisticated essay that I thought would be over her head. The essay was based on themes in Philbrick's book *Mayflower*, a book she would probably never read. He begins his essay: "When we think of the Pilgrims, we think of Thanksgiving and Pilgrim's Rock." The story recounts a battle between the Pilgrims and Native Americans in exciting detail. I asked her teacher if I could come in and share this audio story with the class. The students sat with rapt attention. I played the story only once but they remembered key parts and were able to make inferences beyond the text. I was blown away by their ability to comprehend something that was written for adults. I left feeling very excited about the potential of audio to engage and teach students. And the experience lit a flame of passion for me to take my love of audio into education.

SUPPORTS FOR LISTENING LITERACY

Children are natural listeners. Provided they are not hearing impaired, they are born listening. They are absorbing and learning at all times. Children go to school to learn how to read, one of the most important skills they will learn. Reading is an important predictor of children's success in school, and in college and careers.[3] And yet, teaching listening as a method of developing literacy skills in K–12 schools is largely overlooked. That's despite the fact that listening is linked to both literacy and academic success.[4]

One of the most often cited studies is by Stitch and James, which finds evidence strongly suggesting that children's listening comprehension outpaces reading comprehension until the middle school years (see Figure 5.1).[5] This citation is used by the Common Core ELA standards as a justification for why listening is now an anchor standard of the Common Core. Even states that are not using Common Core standards include listening in their curriculum standards.

Figure 5.1 How listening comprehension outpaces reading comprehension in the early years and remains important to understanding.
Source: Stitch and James.[6]

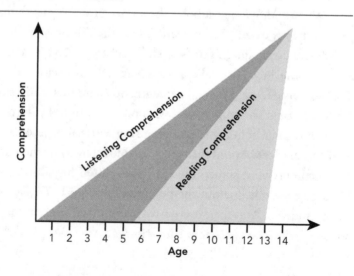

There are demonstrated ways to improve reading through focusing on listening. One method was discovered by Brij Kothari, an Indian academic who was trying to address the high rate of semi-literate and illiterate people in India, where only 74% of people are literate. This is below the global literacy rate for people over 15 years old, which is 85%. This means nearly 1 billion people in India cannot read.[7]

This rate has improved in the last 20 years, in part because Kothari made the connection between listening and reading. Kothari knew that millions of Indians watched Bollywood movies every day and sang along with the catchy lyrics. If those lyrics were also on the screen every time the movie played, viewers would be getting incidental exposure to reading. It's especially effective with these dramatic, repetitive songs, because viewers see words multiple times. Same language subtitling (or SLS) is now implemented on many Bollywood movies on TV because of Kothari's research. Songs are better than all dialogue, Kothari says, because you can anticipate the lyrics and there is a lot of repetition. Kothari, who created the nonprofit Planet Read, has since confirmed his observations in multiple studies. A study conducted by Kothari and other researchers at an Indian primary school found that 10–15% of the children who typically would not have read a grade 5 level text, were able to read it after two years of regular exposure to Bollywood movies with captioning.[8]

Listening and reading together lead to better outcomes. Kothari concluded that "same language subtitling simultaneously makes reading practice an incidental, automatic, and subconscious process."

Using subtitles in videos and reading a transcript while listening have been more commonly used when learning a second language. I remember using this method in the language lab for my middle school French class. We would sit individually with headphones and a tape recorder and listen while reading a story. We had to manually move the tape in reverse or fast forward to repeat a tough section or skip ahead.

This method has moved out of the language lab and into the mainstream classroom (and off the tape recorder and into the cloud) as teachers have realized the benefits of listening and reading together. Listening and reading together allows learners to recognize words, both how they are spelled and pronounced, and hear natural pacing.

In one study, first graders were asked to read along while listening to a story. They were able to detect when a word read aloud was different from the word on the page. Margaret McMahon's research shows that reading and listening together ignite the same cognitive processes and are the same unified task.[9]

For this reason, Listenwise has read-along interactive transcripts for every podcast on the website. While some edtech tools and ebooks have computer-generated audio that accompanies text, it's unusual to find authentic audio with a corresponding interactive transcript in an educational tool. Anecdotally, teachers tell us that they can see how the interactive transcript supports reading.

The Missing Piece of The Literacy Puzzle

Many people think of "literacy" as simply the ability to read. The National Center for Education Statistics defines it as "using printed and written information to function in society, to achieve one's goals, and to develop one's knowledge and potential."[10] But that definition has evolved. Now current literacy theory looks at literacy as integrating the four domains of language: reading, writing, speaking, and listening. The ELA standards in the Common Core say that students should be college ready in reading, writing, speaking and listening, which make up "the literate individual."[11]

> *Studies show a clear relationship between reading and listening.*
> —Timothy Shanahan, Distinguished Professor Emeritus at the University of Illinois at Chicago (retired) and Founding Director of the UIC Center for Literacy

Reading is a crucial skill for the success of your students. That's why so much time and so many resources are devoted to teaching and improving it. And yet, millions of students still struggle to be proficient readers. They exit the early grades, where teaching reading is a focus, and are sometimes silently falling behind because they can't keep up with the reading demands as texts become more difficult. And teachers like you may be struggling with how to help these students.

The consequences of not becoming good readers are serious for those students and the nation. According to the report "Double Jeopardy: How Third-Grade Reading Skills and Poverty Influence High School Graduation," children who are not reading proficiently by the fourth grade are four times more likely to drop out of high school.[12] Multiple studies cited in the report show the personal and economic impacts of not graduating from high school.

I knew these statistics very well because as a reporter for the NPR news station in Boston in 2009, I wrote an award-winning series on the alarmingly elevated high school dropout rate called "Project Dropout." [2] The series chronicled the causes and consequences of not attaining a high school degree. They include a lifetime of lower wages, which means lower tax revenues for communities, and an increase in social services for everything from health coverage to prison costs; 2.1 million high school students dropped out in 2018, the latest year the federal government issued statistics. A high percentage of these students are Hispanic or Black.[13] It is a national tragedy.

It's disheartening to look back at my work and see that I could write almost the same series today about the "crisis" because not much has changed. The struggle in schools often begins when students fail to learn how to read. In the 2019 Nation's Report Card, only 35% of fourth graders performed at or above proficiency on the National Assessment of Educational Progress (NAEP) reading assessment.[14] That's one percentage point lower than in 2017 (see Figure 5.2). Our students are trending backward. And the

Figure 5.2 Fourth-grade student reading scores on the NAEP have only slightly improved over the last decade. *Source:* NAEP Report Card: Reading, The Nation's Report Card.[15]

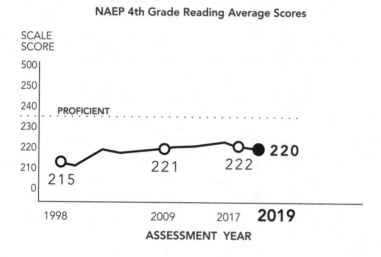

disruption in school due to the coronavirus pandemic is further disrupting students' reading gains.

A reading forecast by the Brookings Institution in the spring of 2020 at the start of the pandemic projected that because of the "COVID slide," students could begin school in the fall of 2020 with only 70% of the learning gains in reading from the prior year.[16]

This most certainly will have an impact on the NAEP scores. Already, after decades of innovations in reading instruction, students' scores have remained essentially flat for more than 20 years.

I believe listening is the missing piece of the literacy puzzle. If we devoted more time to developing students' listening comprehension skills, we could potentially address the gap of the widespread reading deficit.

And it's never too early to start. Reading bedtime stories was always a good way for me to end the day with my children. We were exhausted at the end of the day, ready to rush past the story and get the kids to bed. But we were overlooking all of the important skills we were building with our children while reading to them. The nonprofit Reach Out and Read encourages caregivers to read to their children as infants to prepare them for the literacy journey. Their research shows that reading aloud helps kids recognize sounds and letters, learn new words, become better listeners, and understand how stories work.[17]

> *Read to your kids as long as they will listen to you. You will always be exposing them to vocabulary, language structure, and concepts.*
> —Christin Wheeler, Reading specialist, Brookline, MA

Listening comprehension is a fundamental building block of reading comprehension development. The widely cited "simple view of reading" suggests that reading is a function of two key components: decoding and listening comprehension (see Figure 5.3).[18] Differences in students' reading comprehension performance can be largely predicted by their decoding skills (the process of translating text into pronounceable words) and listening comprehension skills (the ability to make meaning from language). Decoding and listening are necessary, but neither is sufficient alone for a student to be a good reader.

We have ways to measure decoding and listening comprehension separately, so we can look at these different components to better understand a student's reading comprehension scores. In reading, if a student has weak decoding skills but average listening comprehension the child could be struggling with dyslexia.

Figure 5.3 Listening comprehension is a fundamental building block of learning to read.
Source: MetaMetrics.

A student who has average decoding skills and weak listening comprehension skills might be considered a "poor comprehender." Both are poor readers, but for different reasons. If a student is weak in both areas, the student is known as a "garden variety poor reader" (see Figure 5.4).

Figure 5.4 Reading difficulties identified by the simple view. *Source:* Listenwise, adapted from MetaMetrics.

DECODING & LISTENING COMPREHENSION

The "simple model" provides evidence that reading comprehension consists primarily of decoding and listening comprehension.

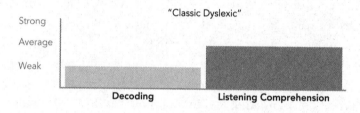

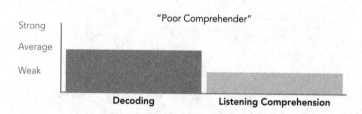

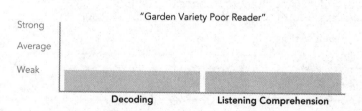

Clear Relationship Between Listening and Reading

As students grow older and improve their decoding skills, the relative importance of listening comprehension skills increases. According to research in the *Journal of Educational Psychology*, listening comprehension explains the unique variations in reading comprehension at grades 3 and 5.[19]

Even though Gough and Tumner's theory of the "simple view of reading" has been supported by years of empirical research, relatively little attention has been given to improving listening comprehension in order to improve reading. But with the more prevalent view of literacy encompassing all four language domains, there is now an increased focus on listening. In addition, the Common Core asks teachers to use technology and digital media "thoughtfully to enhance [students'] reading, writing, speaking, and listening."

Dr. Tiffany Hogan, a researcher at Massachusetts General Hospitals' Institute of Health Professions, found that listening comprehension is the dominating influence on reading comprehension starting in the upper elementary grades.[20] She and her colleagues discovered listening comprehension skills have been shown to be a leading cause of reading difficulties in the fourth grade and older.[21]

Hogan found that, over time, the relative importance of listening comprehension increases as a child becomes a more proficient reader. Decoding is still important to reading comprehension, it's just less of a potential roadblock once kids have mastered it. In fact, by eighth grade, "all of the reliable variance in reading comprehension could be explained by the listening comprehension factor." A child who is a "poor comprehender" can have average decoding skills and thus go undetected as a struggling reader because they can get the gist of a text, make inferences, and understand idioms. But their reading skills are still lacking.

New research by MetaMetrics, the company that created the Lexile Framework for Reading, affirms that as readers develop, the weight of decoding decreases and the weight of listening comprehension increases in predicting reading comprehension. Figure 5.5 illustrates this.

This isn't to say that listening is not important to comprehension in the early grades. In fact, it's extremely important from the youngest ages. However, in the early grades, students are focused on learning to make meaning from words in print, and typically texts they are reading are simple in structure and contain words that are familiar from oral language. It is important to know students' strengths and weaknesses early on, so practicing and testing both listening and decoding skills is key. Poor comprehenders may have intact word decoding capabilities, but their hidden impairment may go unnoticed until later grades when they are faced with more complex academic texts that depart more significantly from their oral language. They tend to fall behind as texts become more conceptually complex, with more academic vocabulary and background knowledge required to understand.

Figure 5.5 Decoding decreases as the weight of listening comprehension increases.
Source: MetaMetrics.

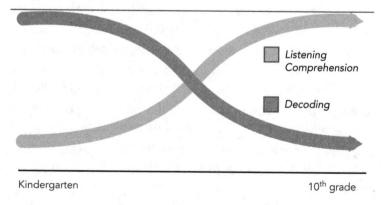

Once a student is in fourth grade, there is more emphasis on reading to learn facts and ideas. Reading instruction typically slows or stops. Many teachers don't know how to help struggling readers. Unless teachers have some background in language or reading instruction, they may be flummoxed by kids who are falling behind because of reading comprehension issues. This is an excellent opportunity to engage students in listening, but one that is often underutilized. When you incorporate more listening into your instructions, you are helping these struggling readers.

Students who have not mastered decoding can still develop language skills by listening to stories and content read aloud. "There is considerable evidence that, for the majority of children, comprehension of printed language continues to lag behind comprehension of spoken language well past third grade (Sticht & James, 1984)," according to Andrew Biemiller, who wrote the *Handbook of Language and Literacy Development*.[22] He cites a number of studies that show, on average, children can't read at the same level as they can listen until around the seventh or eighth grades.

Listening provides a way to improve students' language skills, making complex ideas more accessible to students and exposing them to vocabulary and language patterns that are not part of their everyday speech. For example, students may be able to listen to and understand the plot and character development of Don Quixote and his inner journey, but not be able to decode enough words on their own to make sense of the text while reading.

The National Early Literacy Panel found in 2008 that the correlations between listening and reading comprehension are significant with young children.[23] In a 2018 webinar, literacy expert Timothy Shanahan explained that many studies have shown a large and significant relationship between children's early language development, including listening, and later reading achievement.[24] Given the strong link between listening and reading, it stands to reason that improving listening comprehension skills leads to stronger reading skills. However, there has been a notable lack of research in this area, in part because valid, reliable measures of listening comprehension have been lacking.

With the corollary relationship between listening and reading, there is no need to wait for definitive studies proving the link further. There is a tremendous opportunity with these struggling readers to use more audio-based resources to teach vocabulary, background knowledge, and curriculum content.

My daughter is an example of why reading is so complex and confounds educators. She probably would have benefited from a more focused listening comprehension intervention or regular practice of listening. We stopped the extra reading support in the fifth grade. Her academics improved until she was an A student, so I thought the problem had resolved itself. But her reading difficulties didn't disappear. She has the cognitive intelligence to understand sentence structure and language to make sense of the content. And she is compensating for the phonological processing issues. But she is not the optimal reader she could be.

Listening Is Not Cheating!

With the increasing prevalence of audio books, a heated debate has sprung up in recent years. Is listening to a book cheating? Or is listening to a book the same as reading a book? This question gets to the fundamental similarities and differences between reading and listening.

> *Two thirds of my students felt like hearing stories about an event before reading the textbook helped them understand the event better.*
> —Scott Petri, 10th- and 11th-grade
> History educator, Valencia, CA

We know that reading aloud or listening to podcasts makes complex ideas more accessible and exposes children to vocabulary and language patterns that are not part of everyday speech. This, in turn, helps them understand the structure of books when they read independently. And because reading problems can persist well beyond the elementary grades when reading is typically taught, listening to text, whether in an audio book or a podcast, is easier than reading it for many students.

One study of college-educated adults who were native English speakers were split into three groups and each given a chapter from the novel *Unbroken: A World War II Story of Survival, Resilience, and Redemption* by Laura Hillenbrand.[25] One group listened to a digital audio book. The second group read an e-text. The third group listened to the digital audio book while also reading the e-text. It was not an interactive transcript, so it did not highlight the words as they were spoken. The replaying/fast-forwarding mechanism was disabled. Each group took a 48-question quiz following the chapter. They were asked the same multiple-choice questions online two weeks later.

The result was that participants recalled similar amounts of information, regardless of how they consumed the information—reading, listening, or both. This was a study to register comprehension and retention of information among college-educated adults. But it could be generalized to anyone with well-developed listening and reading comprehension skills. Unfortunately, it did not examine how using literacy supports, such as an interactive transcript, could enhance word recognition and reading fluency. So if the goal is understanding the content of the text, listening is as good as reading. And, in some cases, it may help learners both to access a common text and to develop their reading skills. These are important findings for the future of literacy. For all the focus that's been put on decoding and reading fluency, if more attention were paid to listening, I believe we could help millions of people become better readers.

How to Apply This in Your Classroom

There are multiple ways to focus on listening and reading in your classroom. If you are an elementary school teacher, reading a book aloud while showing students the text is something you probably already do. As students become independent readers, you can encourage them to find audio books in the school or public library. Suggest they check out the print version as well as the audio version and read along while listening. Unfortunately, most audio book platforms do not display the transcripts with the audio. If you teach high school students, you can encourage listening to books as much as you do reading books.

> *I have a couple of students with dyslexia and a couple others with low reading scores who were able to feel successful and not embarrassed by listening to the articles and following along.*
> —Alli Calvert, high school Science teacher,
> Fremont, CA

The interactive transcripts on Listenwise are essentially "same language subtitling" or "closed captioning" for the audio. But it's more precise than subtitling in video. In a video, the standard practice is for the entire sentence or phrases to be displayed at once. In an interactive audio player, the words are highlighted as they are spoken.

A listener can click on a word in the transcript and jump to that position in the audio. Or you can slide the play head along in the story and the transcript will follow. This method is also highly motivating. Students don't feel that reading is a burden. This is documented in multiple studies. Reading while listening increases motivation and is automatic and subconscious. In one study, the reading-while-listening group "resulted in twice the amount of reading" as the control group and "led to higher scores on listening comprehension measures."[26]

Class Activity: Using the Interactive Transcript

All NPR stories have transcripts available on the internet. But a printed PDF isn't as useful as an interactive tool that highlights the words as they are spoken. For that reason, I recommend you go to https://listenwise.com/book and sign up for a trial of Listenwise Premium to use the interactive transcripts for the following exercises.

Elementary Students: For this activity, you must be able to project your computer screen. Select a story that aligns with your curriculum. As an example, I will use an episode from the podcast *But Why* with a lesson on Listenwise called "Garbage in the Sea." [3]

Before Listening: Begin the lesson by asking students to raise their hands if they have used any of the following: disposable plastic straws, plastic juice or water bottles, or plastic bags. Ask them what these items have in common (made of plastic, typically used one time only). Tell them that, of the millions of tons of plastic items produced every year, about half of them are used just once and then thrown away, and sometimes they end up in the ocean. Ask students to guess what problems might result when plastic straws, water bottles, and plastic bags end up in the ocean (fish get caught, sea animals eat them, they never decompose).

Preview the vocabulary by reading aloud the terms and their definitions. In this story, the words you focus on when reading along with the transcript include activist, gyre, concentrated, and fragments. The definitions are provided on Listenwise.

During Listening: Project the transcript as the story plays. When students see or hear the vocabulary word in the story, ask them to raise their hands. Stop the story, click on the word, and replay the phrases around it at least two times. Demonstrating the interactive transcript shows students how to build both their listening comprehension and decoding skills. It also allows them to hear the word authentically spoken in a meaningful academic context.

To reinforce comprehension, click on the "Slower" button in the upper right hand above the audio bar. Play the same sentence again with the key vocabulary word to ensure all students understand.

After Listening: Ask students to discuss the listening comprehension questions with a partner and then share their responses with the group. Check for understanding, replaying segments of audio where relevant information can be found.

Middle/High School Students: Select a lesson from Listenwise that corresponds with your teaching goals. Prepare to project the interactive transcript at the front of the class or make sure to assign the listening with the interactive transcript if teaching remote. Before listening preview the vocabulary, during listening stop and replay challenging words or phrases, after listening pair up students to discuss the listening comprehension questions with a partner and then share their responses with the group. Discuss how reading the transcript along with the listening enhanced students' understanding of the text.

Building Vocabulary and Reading Fluency

Several studies show an important connection between reading and listening comprehension and building vocabulary and reading fluency. One study of third graders found that vocabulary and word reading fluency were found to contribute to both reading and listening comprehension.[27] Understanding vocabulary is a key component of literacy, whether you are listening or reading. Vocabulary is one of the most important predictors of success. This is true for both beginning readers and English language learners.

Reading fluency is a key instructional goal, and thus it's important to understand how Reading While Listening (RWL) impacts fluency. A study of third graders using a RWL app showed improvement over the control group.[28] The study showed a significant word count per minute improvement in the treatment group compared to the control group. These are promising results, but more study is needed.

Sadly, there are limited studies that look closely at how listening comprehension and reading are connected and the instructional implications of that relationship. It is my hope that, with the introduction of the Lexile Framework for Listening, which I discuss in another chapter, there will be more research into how improving listening can improve reading.

―――――――――――――――●―――――――――――――――

Class Activity: Identifying Main Idea

Strategy in Brief: This strategy helps to engage students in listening to identify the main idea of a story. The Directed Listening Thinking Activity (DLTA) guides students in making and confirming predictions about the story and then summarizing those ideas.[29]

Rationale: The ability to make and confirm predictions is an important comprehension strategy. It helps students to determine the speaker's main points and to pay attention and stay focused when listening. The DLTA affords students with this opportunity, calling on them to make predictions before, during, and after the listening experience. Discussion happens at all three phases as well, so students have time to learn from others and adjust their predictions if necessary. The ability to put clues together to infer the speaker's main idea is another essential listening comprehension skill. Stopping at various points and thinking about what they have heard can also help students identify the main idea. If students use what they know and continue to learn through the listening experience, they will better understand the speaker's main idea.

Middle/High School Students: This activity should be used with the NPR story "Trapped Miners Face Dangerous Isolation." [4]

Before Listening: State the objective: "The purpose of today's lesson is to help you better comprehend an audio story by making and confirming predictions when listening. You will show your understanding by answering oral and written questions." Instruct students to fold a piece of paper into four parts.

Number each part 1–4. Select photos from the internet of a coal miner. Say to students: "Here is a photo that has something to do with the story you will be listening to today. Based on this picture, what do you predict it will be about? Write your prediction in box 1.

Show the photos. After giving students time to write a brief response, allow them to pair and share, saying, "Turn to the person next to you and share one of your ideas." Show the words listed below on a display large enough for all to see. Say, "Here are some words you will hear as you listen to the audio story." Be sure to take time to read them together with students.

- miner
- resilient
- diversion
- predicament
- diversity

Say, "Based on these words, now what do you predict the audio story might say about the miners? Write your prediction in box 2." Again, if time allows, have students pair and share.

Say, "The title of today's audio story is "Trapped Chilean Miners Face Dangerous Isolation." Based on the photos you've seen, the words we've read, and the title of the audio story, what do you think the audio story might tell you about? Write your prediction in box 4." Again, if time allows, have students pair and share.

During Listening: Have students turn over their papers and make two columns by drawing a vertical line in the middle. They will use it as a listening guide. Have students label one column "My Predictions" and the other "Professor's Ideas."

Say, "Today you will be listening to an interview between a reporter and Professor Lawrence Palinkas, a professor of social policy and health at the University of Southern California. Based on the photos, words, and title of this audio story, what do you think he will say about how the miners are reacting to being trapped? Write your prediction in the first column. As you listen, capture as much as you can about what the professor says, and write his ideas in the column next to yours, titled 'Professor's Ideas.' At the end of the segment, we will stop and summarize what you thought the professor might say and what he actually said." You should allow the students to see the transcript as well and follow along with the audio. Being able to summarize after each segment will help students figure out the main point the speaker is trying to make in this audio story.

Play audio from beginning to 1:11 and stop. Say, "So how well do your predictions match with what the professor stated?" Give students time to check.

Say, "In this next segment, the professor says that certain patterns of behavior will emerge, which will enable the minors to survive. What do you think these might be? Write your ideas in section 2 in the 'My Predictions' column."

Play audio from 1:11 to 2:24 and stop. Say, "So, how well do your predictions match with what the professor stated?" Give students time to check.

Say, "In the next part, the interviewer asks if the miners should be medicated. How do you think the professor will respond: yes or no? Write your predictions in the third section in the 'My Predictions' column."

Play audio to 3:00 and stop. Say, "So how well do your predictions match with what the professor stated?" Give students time to check.

Explain, "In this last section, the professor explains why the miners might survive. What characteristics do you think he will mention? Write your ideas in the fourth section of your listening guide."

Play audio until the end of the story. Say, "So how well do your predictions match with what the professor stated? What kind of attributes did he mention?" Give students time to check.

After Listening: Ask a question such as: "Now that you have heard this entire interview, what would you say is the main idea for the audience to take away from this audio story?"

Say, "Let's now revisit your initial predictions. Turn your paper over and look through your predictions. Look for how they might have changed." After giving students time to take a look, say something such as, "If your predictions changed, what caused you to make changes?" The main point to elicit is that listeners often change their predictions as they gain more information, and that's what they should do. It shows that they are attending to what is being said and altering their own ideas as needed.

Elementary Students: Adapt the above activity to use with the NPR story "Killer Whale Who Carried Dead Calf 2 Years Ago Is Pregnant Again." [5]

This activity is from Listenwise's Literacy Coach's Toolkit,[30] which can be found at https://listenwise.com/book.

My daughter, the struggling reader, is now in her senior year in high school. She is an A student and in the National Honor Society. I often forget she can't read fluently. But when she reads something out loud, whether it's a sentence from an app on her phone or directions to a game, she stumbles over her words. She is still not decoding properly.

It has been by sheer determination and a lot of inferencing and background knowledge that she succeeds. As she heads to college, we've realized she needs to have this problem addressed. She is now using an adaptive reading fluency program to continue to practice her reading skills. And she is listening to a lot of audio books and podcasts.

Her academic future has not been hampered by her reading struggles, but I know she is lucky in that regard. And I think about how much more she will learn and contribute when she becomes a more fluent reader.

REFLECTION AND PLANNING

Take this opportunity to write some reflections and plans for action.

To better understand your readers, think about your students who struggle to read. Do a quick assessment in your mind about whether they might be a "Classic Dyslexic," "Poor Comprehender," or "Garden Variety Poor Reader." How might listening help that reader?

Write down a list of ways you can quickly introduce Reading While Listening in your classroom. This could be with a read-aloud book, an audio book, or Listenwise.

_____

_____

How will you teach vocabulary through listening?

_____

_____

Audio Resources

[1] Philbrick, Nathaniel. (2006, November 22). Debunking Pilgrim myths: Before Plymouth. NPR, www.npr.org/templates/story/story.php?storyId=6526328.

[2] Brady-Myerov, Monica. (2009, March 9). Project dropout: Does the MCAS cause students to drop out? | WBUR, www.wbur.org/news/2009/03/09/project-dropout-does-the-mcas-cause-students-to-drop-out.

[3] Lindholm, Jane, & Melody Bodette. (2019, February 15). Why is there a big patch of garbage in the Pacific ocean? Vermont Public Radio, www.vpr.org/post/why-there-big-patch-garbage-pacific-ocean.

[4] Simon, Scott. (2010, August 28). Trapped miners face dangerous isolation. NPR, www.npr.org/templates/story/story.php?storyId=129492511.

[5] Shapiro, Ari, & Ailsa Chang. (2020, July 28). Killer whale who carried dead calf 2 years ago is pregnant again. NPR, www.npr.org/2020/07/28/896334970/killer-whale-who-carried-dead-calf-2-years-ago-is-pregnant-again.

References

1. Brigman, G., Lane, D., Switzer, D., Lane, D., & Lawrence, R. (1999). Teaching children school success skills. _Journal of Educational Research, 92_(6), 323–329. doi:10.1080/00220679909597615.

2. Hogan, T., Adlof, S.M., & Alonzo, C.N. (2014). On the importance of listening comprehension. *International Journal of Speech-Language Pathology, 16*(3): 199–207.

3. Spörer, N., & Brunstein, J.C. (2009). Fostering the reading comprehension of secondary school students through peer-assisted learning: Effects on strategy knowledge, strategy use, and task performance. *Contemporary Educational Psychology, 34*(4), 289–297. doi:10.1016/j.cedpsych .2009.06.004.

4. Beall, M.L., Gill-Rosier, J., Tate, J., & Matten, A. (2008). State of the context: Listening in education. *International Journal of Listening, 22*(2), 123–132. doi:10.1080 /10904010802174826.

5. Sticht, T.G., & James, J.H. (1984). Listening and reading. In P.D. Pearson, R. Barr, M.L. Kamil, & P. Mosenthal (Eds.), *Handbook of reading research* (Vol. 1, pp. 293–317). White Plains, NY: Longman.

6. Ibid.

7. Plecher, P. (2020, July 22). India—Literacy rate 2018. https:// www.statista.com/statistics/271335/literacy-rate-in-india/ (accessed September 21, 2020).

8. Kothari, B., Takeda, J., Joshi, A., & Pandey, A. (2002). Same language subtitling: A butterfly for literacy? *International Journal of Lifelong Education, 21*(1), 55–66. doi:10.1080 /02601370110099515.

9. Mcmahon, M.L. (1983). Development of reading-while-listening skills in the primary grades. *Reading Research Quarterly, 19*(1), 38. doi:10.2307/747336.

10. National Center for Education Statistics. (2020). National Assessment of Adult Literacy (NAAL). https://nces.ed.gov/ NAAl/fr_definition.asp (accessed September 21, 2020).

11. Common Core State Standards Initiative. (n.d.). English language arts standards. Introduction. Students who

are college and career ready in reading, writing, speaking, listening, & language. http://www.corestandards.org/ELA-Literacy/introduction/students-who-are-college-and-career-ready-in-reading-writing-speaking-listening-language/ (accessed September 21, 2020).

12. Hernandez, D.J. (2012). *Double jeopardy: How third-grade reading skills and poverty influence high school graduation* (pp. 1–21, Rep.). Baltimore, MD: Annie E. Casey Foundation.

13. The NCES Fast Facts Tool Provides Quick Answers to Many Education Questions (National Center for Education Statistics)." *National Center for Education Statistics (NCES) Home Page, a Part of the U.S. Department of Education,* nces.ed.gov/fastfacts/display.asp?id=16.

14. The Nation's Report Card. (n.d.). NAEP report card: Reading. https://www.nationsreportcard.gov/reading/nation/achievement/?grade=4 (accessed September 21, 2020).

15. Sticht, T.G., & James, J.H. (1984). Listening and reading. In P.D. Pearson, R. Barr, M.L. Kamil, & P. Mosenthal (Eds.), *Handbook of reading research* (pp. 255–292). New York, NY: Longman.

16. Soland, J., Kuhfeld, M., Tarasawa, B., Johnson, A., Ruzek, E., & Liu, J. (2020, May 27). The impact of COVID-19 on student achievement and what it may mean for educators. Brookings, https://www.brookings.edu/blog/brown-center-chalkboard/2020/05/27/the-impact-of-covid-19-on-student-achievement-and-what-it-may-mean-for-educators/ (accessed September 21, 2020).

17. Reach Out and Read. (2019, November 18). Child development. https://reachoutandread.org/why-we-matter/child-development/ (accessed September 21, 2020).

18. Gough, P.B., & Tunmer, W.E. (1986). Decoding, reading, and reading disability. *Remedial and Special Education, 7*(1), 6–10. doi:10.1177/074193258600700104.

19. Berninger, V.W., & Abbott, R.D. (2010). Listening comprehension, oral expression, reading comprehension, and written expression: Related yet unique language systems in grades 1, 3, 5, and 7. *Journal of Educational Psychology, 102*(3), 635–651. https://doi.org/10.1037/a0019319.

20. Hogan, T., Adlof, S.M., & Alonzo, C.N. (2014). On the importance of listening comprehension. *International Journal of Speech-Language Pathology, 16*(3), 199–207.

21. Catts, H.W., Hogan, T.P., & Adlof, S.M. (2005). Developmental changes in reading and reading disabilities. In H.W. Catts & A.G. Kamhi (Eds.), *The Connections Between Language and Reading Disabilities* (pp. 25–40). Mahwah, NJ: Lawrence Erlbaum.

22. Biemiller, A. (2014, October 30). Oral comprehension sets the ceiling on reading comprehension. American Federation of Teachers, https://www.aft.org/periodical/american-educator/spring-2003/oral-comprehension-sets-ceiling-reading (accessed September 21, 2020).

23. Shanahan, T. (Chair). (n.d.). *Developing early literacy: A scientific synthesis of early literacy development and implications for intervention* (pp. 1–260, Rep.). National Early Literacy Panel.

24. Listenwise (Producer). (2018). *Listening and reading* [Webinar] https://www.youtube.com/watch?v=YlVpgDAUpPw (accessed September 21, 2020).

25. Rogowsky, B.A., Calhoun, B.M., & Tallal, P. (2016). Does modality matter? The effects of reading, listening, and dual modality on comprehension. *SAGE Open, 6*(3). doi:10.1177/2158244016669550.

26. Shany, M., & Biemiller, A. (1995). Assisted reading practice: Effects on performance for poor readers in grades 3 and 4. *Reading Research Quarterly, 30*, 382. doi:10.2307/747622.

27. Wolf, M.C., Muijselaar, M.M.L., Boonstra, A.M., & de Bree, E.H. (2019). The relationship between reading and listening comprehension: Shared and modality-specific components. *Read Writ, 32*, 1747–1767. https://doi.org/10.1007/s11145-018-9924-8.

28. Friedland, A., Gilman, M., Johnson, M., & Ambaye, A.D. (2017). Does reading-while-listening enhance students' reading fluency? Preliminary results from school experiments in rural Uganda. *Journal of Education and Practice, 8*, 82–95.

29. Stauffer, R.G. (1980). *The language-experience approach to the teaching of reading.* New York, NY: Harper & Row.

30. Listenwise. (Producer). (2018). *Listenwise literacy coach's toolkit.* https://support.listenwise.com/wp-content/uploads/2019/01/Listenwise-Literacy-Coachs-Toolkit.pdf.

Chapter 6

English Learners and Listening

Vicki worries most about one boy in her class. His name is Hassan and he joined her class just before Thanksgiving when his family immigrated from Syria. She doesn't know much about him except that he lived in a refugee camp in Turkey with his family before coming to the United States.

Hassan has some English language skills he learned before leaving Syria, but he's shy about speaking in English. If he doesn't learn English quickly, however, he won't be able to meet the demands of her classroom. While he is getting pull-out ESL instruction, Vicki knows she also has to prepare her lessons so he can participate.

Every year there are several children like Hassan in her classroom: children who enter mid-year with limited English skills. Some move from their home country, others have missed years of school because they have been refugees, living far from home sometimes in refugee camps. And there are other children of immigrants who were born in the United States but still struggle with English because they only speak their first language at home. Vicki is not a certified English as a Second Language teacher. She has taken the required hours of professional development to scaffold her lessons for English learners, but it takes time and expertise she doesn't have.

Vicki thinks about the moments in her class when Hassan is captivated, fully paying attention. They are in circle time, listening to a story read aloud. Or in one-on-one conversations. Listening is obviously key to his understanding of English. She needs to find ways to bring more listening to English into her teaching.

LANGUAGE LEARNING AND LISTENING

Like most students, I was required to learn a foreign language in middle school. For me, it was French. I think that was one of two languages offered at my public school in Lexington, Kentucky in 1980. I could never get used to how it sounded or how I sounded trying to speak it. While I did okay in the class, I didn't discover a love of languages. And although I tried to learn French again in college, I didn't succeed. The experience really didn't give me an understanding of what it's like to live in another country where I don't speak the language, surrounded by people with whom I need to communicate but can't. That feeling of confusion, isolation, misunderstanding, and frustration—that came later.

As a sophomore in college, I chose to study for a semester in Kenya because Kenyan family friends were journalists in Nairobi and they invited me to spend the summer in a journalism internship. I thought it would be a good idea to first do a study abroad program in Kenya to better understand the history and culture of a country I had never visited. There was one downside: a program requirement to learn Swahili.

I had little faith in my language abilities after trying to learn French, but the Swahili language portion of the program was a truly immersive experience. Our student group lived on Lamu, an island off the Northern coast of Kenya, where Swahili is the primary language spoken. For one month, we studied nothing but Swahili language and culture. I quickly learned that a key element to learning any second language is listening. It was the main focus of our language study. In just a few weeks, I became conversational in Swahili and easily passed the requirement.

Millions of students in our K–12 public schools are on an island of sorts where English is the primary language, but the education system is not designed to help them become fluent in English. They must learn the basic mechanics and vocabulary of the English language in addition to the content of math, science, social studies, and ELA.

According to data from the National Center for Education Statistics, in 2017 10% of students in public schools were classified as English language learners or ELs. The distribution of these students is not even;[1] 21% of all urban public school students are ELs. It is the fastest-growing population of students in the United States and is expected to continue to grow. The National Education Association projects that by 2025 one out of every four public school students will be an English learner.[2]

Understanding and incorporating more listening activities into your instruction can help this important, growing segment of school children. We know that listening is essential to learning a language. Whether you are a general education teacher, ESL teacher, or bilingual educator, implementing more listening activities, across content areas, can help all of your students. Remember, 80% of what we learn, we learn through listening.[3] If you work to build solid listening skills to help your ELs, you will be helping all of your students.

How many times have you heard someone who is learning a new language say "I can understand more than I can speak." It's widely accepted that students cannot learn to speak another language without focusing on listening comprehension. Listening and understanding another language precedes speaking in the second language and helps students learn the rules, the syntax and grammar, of the new language. Speaking and listening go hand in hand. It makes sense to give your language students more listening activities to build their speaking skills.

Just like listening in one's first language, listening comprehension in a second language involves low-level and high-level processes. We all receive information in a variety of ways, using all of our senses. Our brain then processes the information and we produce our understanding of the information we've received. We could do this by speaking, writing, or making something.

For English learners, receptive language, or understanding what is heard, comes more quickly and easily than expressive language, or producing speech. In between receiving and expressing information is processing. Those of us who speak English as our first language do it without thinking about it. Research has shown that there are two types of processing. Low-level processing happens quickly and automatically. It's like conversational language. I see a car drive by, I know it's a car. I might say, "I saw a blue car drive by my house."

In high-level processing, a person accesses background knowledge and context to understand the meaning of words and sentences. The knowledge is stored in long-term memory. For instance, if I listen to the NPR story "Glossy View of the Soviet Era Takes Hold in Russia," I need to understand the Bolshevik Revolution. [1] But if I don't know what Bolshevism is, I can listen to the context of the story to learn that it was a dictatorship, and use my knowledge of dictatorships and how dictators rule countries to understand the story. All of this must happen very quickly.

> *What an amazing learning experience my mixed level and ELL students have had using Listenwise! They have developed stronger listening skills and used these skills toward comprehension. Having the transcript has been so valuable in supporting literacy for all levels of students.*
>
> —Sarah Emery, grades 5–12 teacher,
> St. Johnsbury, VT

If a learner can't process quickly enough, if they can't understand the meaning of the words or at least the key words in the sentence, they won't be able to access the high-level background knowledge processing required of academic listening comprehension.

Using visual aids is also key to helping students understand a new language. Showing photos, graphics, slides, posters, and other visual representations of the words that students will be hearing can help with comprehension.

According to a study on the types of training that improve learners' second language listening comprehension, researchers found it's critical for language learners that low-level processes happen automatically, because when listening, there's often no opportunity to go back and review something again.[4] Continually incoming speech must be processed immediately. Otherwise, the low-level processing will take up too much attention and prevent the student from accessing their background knowledge or making connections to activate high-level processing. The study warns this may "considerably impair comprehension."

How can you help students improve their listening comprehension while learning English? I suggest using the following five practices focused on listening:

Five Key Practices to Help English Learners Use Listening

1. Preteaching vocabulary
2. Activating prior knowledge and building background knowledge
3. Teaching language and content together
4. Scaffolding instruction for listening
5. Encouraging speaking practice to deepen listening comprehension

Some of you may already have strategies to support your multilingual learners because you teach ELs every day. Others are content teachers facing a variety of language proficiency levels in your classes. Or maybe you teach elementary students with a handful of ELs who receive pull-out sheltered English instruction. The good news is that any one of these practices for improving language acquisition through listening is effective for general education students as well.

English learners in our schools are assessed yearly on their progress and will not graduate without English proficiency. WIDA released a new set of English Language Development Standards in 2020 that "represent the social, instructional, and academic language that students need to engage with peers, educators, and the curriculum in schools."[5] Currently 40 states follow the WIDA standards and administer the ACCESS test once a year to all ELs to determine their progress. States like California and Texas have developed their own tests for English learners. The test covers the four domains: reading, writing, speaking, and listening; 25% of the test involves audio listening. The test is primarily administered online, which means there are no facial cues or gestures to support listening comprehension. English learners in states that don't follow WIDA also are tested regularly. Preparing your students for the rigor of these tests, while also teaching them content, can be supported through listening exercises.

I've broken the five key practices into three stages of listening strategies that can be used with any audio source. We use this instructional framework to structure our Listenwise lessons.

Before Listening

1. Preteaching vocabulary
2. Activating prior knowledge and building background knowledge
3. Teaching language and content together

During Listening

4. Scaffolding instruction for listening
   - Audio transcripts, slower speed, and close listening protocols
   - Listening organizers (language identification)

After Listening

5. Encouraging speaking practice to deepen listening comprehension
   - Conversations for listening comprehension checks

BEFORE LISTENING

In this section, we review activities students can do either on their own in a remote or blended setting or with teacher guidance in the classroom. These activities should happen before listening to the podcast.

Preteaching Vocabulary

English learners often start school behind their peers who speak English fluently. It starts with vocabulary. The average kindergartner knows at least 5,000 words, but while the average EL may know at least 5,000 words in their first language, they know far fewer in English.[6] This leads to a well-documented achievement gap for ELs. A 2014 report by ChildTrend.org comparing scores between EL and non-EL students on the National Assessment of Educational Progress found a 40-percentage-point gap in both fourth-grade reading and eighth-grade math scores. The report notes this chasm has remained unchanged since 2000.[7]

We are asking a lot of our English learners, as they are often reclassified too early in their education journeys. They are moved into general education classes without having fully acquired the academic language and literacy skills they need and must now develop them as they simultaneously learn and apply content area concepts in the second language.

WIDA defines three dimensions of academic language, Word/ Phrase, Sentence, and Discourse. The Before, During, and After listening strategies I've outlined can support all three dimensions.

Although students develop the communication skills necessary for social interactions, such as talking and listening to their peers, they take longer to acquire the vocabulary of academic language. These are terms that are traditionally used in reading, writing, class lectures, debates, and discussions, presentations, speeches, and so on. According to a study by Stanford University, English proficiency can take four to seven years to develop.[8]

Class Activity: Building Vocabulary Comprehension with Close Listening Practice

Elementary School Students: Use the NPR story "Dog Has a Fondness for the Porch at Family's Previous Residence," [2] which is about 30 seconds long. Preview the vocabulary: familiar, traveled, resident, recently, lounging, reunited, current, traveled (they appear in the story in this order). Play the story once through without stopping. On the next play, ask students to raise their hands when they hear one of the vocabulary words. In the final play, stop when it comes to a vocabulary word and ask students to explain its definition and use in the story.

Middle/High School Students: Use the NPR story "Lois Lowry Says 'The Giver' Was Inspired By Her Father's Memory Loss" [3] with your students who are intermediate to advanced English speakers. If you have lower-level students, you could use the story selected for elementary students as the subject matter is fun for everyone.

In this exercise, you will use close listening practice to build vocabulary knowledge using a derivation chart:

Derivation Chart

Determine the noun form of each adjective or adverb and explain how you figured it out.

Noun Word Is Derived From	Suffix
dystopian	
orderly	
colorless	
controversial	

Noun Word Is Derived From	Suffix
bankable	
futuristic	
artfully	
carefully	

Audio and additional resources for this activity can also be found at https://listenwise.com/book.

Everyday basic interpersonal communication skills, known as BICS, are more easily acquired by watching TV, playing video games, or talking with friends. Cognitive academic language proficiency, known as CALP, is required to succeed academically and includes academic language.

Academic language is not just about vocabulary. It's about grammar, syntax, and other language elements. Jeff Zwiers, a Senior Researcher in the Stanford Graduate School of Education, says that while researchers believe reading is the number one way to build academic language, "listening can help build language facility and the sentence variety muscles."

"When listening, you are not as hampered by the decoding process," Zwiers told me in an interview. "Some kids are so hung up on saying the words correctly, that they don't do the comprehension piece. But if you are just listening, you don't have that extra dimension to deal with, it's focusing on the language."

Using podcasts can be powerful because students can listen to the academic language multiple times. Zwiers suggests assigning students to listen to four podcasts on a similar topic because that would reinforce vocabulary and sentence structures that would help build language. He says it's also important to have a purpose for listening, giving students a reason to listen for ideas they can build on and use in other contexts.

Podcasts that are written and produced reports or stories, such as NPR features, would provide students with richer academic language than podcasts that are unscripted, Zweir notes. Unscripted podcasts or interviews use more BICS than CALPS. Podcasts are also excellent for building social language.

Oral language skills and word recognition when listening are the foundation for the development of the more advanced language skills needed for academic comprehension. Listening to stories on a variety of topics provides students with exposure to a wide variety of academic language. It has been shown that incidental exposure to vocabulary through listening to stories helps students learn the meaning of unknown words.[9] When students listen, they hear difficult vocabulary that stretches their receptive abilities, which helps their language acquisition.

Without this crucial academic vocabulary, the words and phrases that serve as the building blocks of language, ELs have a difficult time grasping the increasingly complex concepts presented to them as they learn new concepts and tackle tougher content. Once students are in middle or high school, they are expected to learn more difficult subjects, often without the prerequisite language proficiency or the scaffolding to support their learning needs. The goal of college readiness remains out of reach for many. Fortunately, there's an effective way to help EL students bridge this gap—and it involves preteaching vocabulary before listening.

> *My students feel like the audio stories on Listenwise help them understand the academic vocabulary better.*
> —Scott Petri, high school History teacher,
> Valencia, CA

Preteaching vocabulary is a reading strategy that focuses on teaching students the words they are about to read. There is extensive research showing how important preteaching vocabulary is to reading success. Miller and Veatch in their book

Teaching Literacy in Context demonstrate that this preteaching strategy improves student comprehension.[10] But it is also key to listening comprehension.

Research with young adults in Iran found that emphasizing vocabulary knowledge with both low-level English students and those at the advanced level "positively influences better listening comprehension."[11]

Previewing the vocabulary gets students tuned into what they should be listening for and focusing on. It's especially important if students are one-way listening, which means they are not responding but just passively listening to audio, such as a podcast or a recorded story.

Beck, McKeown, and Kucan classify vocabulary using three "tiers."[12] Tier 1 words are words that are frequently used in English conversation and probably known in the first language of students. They commonly appear in oral language. "Bike" and "happy" are examples of Tier 1 words. Tier 2 and Tier 3 vocabulary words take more time for students to develop than social language. Tier 2 words include academic language frequently used in different contexts across disciplines. They are important for listening comprehension. For instance, the words "respect" and "consequence" are Tier 2 words. Tier 2 also includes phrases such as "in conclusion," which are important signposts for language learners to understand.

Tier 3 words are used less frequently in speech and are often specific to the context of a story. The words are key to understanding the discipline-specific concepts in English. Tier 3 words such as "authoritarian" and "amendment" are important to understanding social studies concepts that are important to the curriculum. Another category of vocabulary is collocations, which are a pair or group of words, such as "take a nap" or "easy money." Even though students can learn the meaning of unknown words through incidental exposure when listening, the vocabulary that is critical for educational success, academic vocabulary, should be a part of your preteaching before listening.

Class Activity: Developing BICS and CALPS

Scripted podcasts include rich academic language that combines BICS and CALPS. These stories often contain many Tier 2 words, as well as many collocations and idioms necessary to understand spoken English.

Elementary School Students: Use the 30-second story from NPR "Alligator Pool Floatie Surprises Florida Couple." [4] In just a few seconds there are several Tier 2 vocabulary words to preview and focus on. Begin by previewing the vocabulary. Play the story multiple times to ensure comprehension.

Tier 2 Vocabulary
   responded
   threatening
   impressively
   realistic
   wrangled
   predator
   deflated

Middle/High School Students: The NPR story "Homeland Security Remains An Agency In Progress," [5] is only 4:22 and has both Tier 2 and 3 words and phrases.

Tier 2 Vocabulary
   existential (adj)
   resiliency (n)
   personnel (n)
   manifest (v)
   conceivable (adj)

Tier 3 Vocabulary (Discipline-specific)
   Islamic extremists (n)
   hurricane (n)
   FEMA (acronym/noun)
   bureaucracy (n)

Tier 3 Vocabulary (Collocations and Idioms)
   "stand alone"
   "with the idea of"
   "a lot of credit"
   "up off its feet"

"come to gel"
"Yeoman's work"
"a work in progress"
"the least of Homeland Securities' worries"
"taking risk into account"
"put to good use"

Using authentic nonfiction news podcasts for improving vocabulary is very effective because there are a large number of Tier 2 words that naturally occur in the stories. In one four-minute story about politics and an upcoming election, the website achievethecore.org found 74 academic words for a sixth-grade student. The words include on grade level words such as "culture" and "inequality" and above grade level words such as "demographic" and "universal" as defined by achievethecore.org.

Activating Prior Knowledge and Building Background Knowledge

In addition to vocabulary, a key element of listening comprehension, especially in learning a second language, is background knowledge of the subject.[13] For English learners who are new to the country, understanding what tennis is versus baseball, could be key to their understanding a reading or listening passage on a language test. Activating students' knowledge about a subject could include asking questions about a topic to elicit what they know, or showing them pictures of people, places, or things mentioned in the story. If students have background knowledge related to the story, activating that knowledge and discussing their own experiences can enhance understanding.

I know first-hand how difficult it is to be dropped into a country and not be able to speak the language. After my failure to learn French and my reluctance to learn Swahili, I thought my language learning days were over when I returned to college from my study abroad in Kenya. I selected a major in international relations, as I wanted to pursue a career as an international radio journalist. There was one problem: To complete the major, I had to be proficient in a foreign language. My one semester of Swahili wasn't enough, and the university didn't offer Swahili in its language department for me to further my studies. I had to learn a new language.

At this point, I had more confidence that I could learn another language. But I wasn't prepared for how long it would take me to truly master it. I chose to learn Portuguese because I wanted to work in Africa as a journalist and Portuguese is one of the major languages spoken in Africa.

I struggled through two years of intensive Portuguese and barely opened my mouth to speak. Most of my classmates had studied abroad in Brazil and had a fluency with the language that I lacked. I did excel at reading and writing in Portuguese and was able to fulfill the language graduation requirement without really learning how to speak Portuguese. After college I worked in Nairobi, Kenya for two years as a freelance radio reporter. I decided to move my operation to Rio de Janeiro, Brazil, but when I arrived I was shocked to learn I couldn't actually speak Portuguese.

I focused on listening first. I listened to the radio, TV news, and Brazilian soap operas to help me understand Portuguese. The nightly soap operas, or "novelas," were especially helpful because there were a limited number of characters and a slow-moving story line. And the story lines are juicy. For example, a daughter killed in a car accident turns out not to be dead but in hiding, and she returns to wreak havoc on her family. But I had no background information. I couldn't figure out what was going on in each scene.

I enlisted my Canadian friend, who was fluent in Portuguese, to give me the necessary background information and some basic vocabulary to improve my understanding. He explained to me the central idea of the story was betrayal. I would pause the show when they discussed the betrayal. I wrote down the words

I couldn't understand. I asked my friend for more guidance. With that basic understanding of the premise of the show, my listening comprehension greatly improved. And with my background knowledge of simple words like daughter, wife, and love, I started to understand. I also hired a Portuguese teacher and started relearning verb tenses and written Portuguese again. But I credit my soap opera watching with making my accent, expressions, and vocabulary sound like a true Brazilian.

Class Activity: Activating Prior Knowledge

Elementary/Middle School Students: Use the podcast about *Tuck Everlasting*. [6] An edited version of the audio and a full lesson can also be found at https://listenwise.com/book.

Activate prior knowledge: Begin the lesson by asking students if they have heard of the Fountain of Youth (a mythical spring—those who drink from it stay young forever). Tell students that for hundreds of years, people have been searching for this fountain but no one has found it. Use the following questions to guide a class or small group discussion: Why do so many people want to stay young? Do you think it is better to be young than old? What messages tell you being young is better than being old (TV commercials, sporting events, news coverage)? What are some things people do to try to look and feel young (exercise, plastic surgery, make-up, hair dye)?

Building background knowledge: A series of images would be a great place to start generating both questions and ideas about what the Fountain of Youth is. A short video could help answer questions and also encourage further wonderings and provide a platform to teach vocabulary. Another idea would be to provide students a series of short sentences containing essential background information to go along with those images or videos.

High School Students: In this activity you can use the NPR story "Toni Morrison's 'Good' Ghosts." [7]

Activate prior knowledge: You first want to find out what your learners know about Toni Morrison. Open class by asking students if they have heard of Toni Morrison. Perhaps look at portions of her bio page. Explain that Morrison is a novelist who writes predominantly about the lives of African Americans, from the era of slavery to contemporary America. Many of her novels are told from the points of view of dead characters. For example, her novel *Beloved*, about two slaves who fall in love, is narrated by the ghost of one of the main characters. The themes of African American life and the afterlife are frequently combined in her work. She won the Nobel Prize for Literature in 1993.

Building background knowledge: Next, especially for ELs, you want to give them the information they need to know to understand the story. Students should know that Toni Morrison was a famous and well-respected African American author whose novels explore the challenges and issues of racism. The novels mentioned in this audio story are *Beloved, Jazz, Song of Solomon,* and *Sula.* It will also help students to know something about slavery in order to understand the political basis of Morrison's work. There are many resources on slavery in the United States available on multiple websites. You can choose to watch a video, read a text, or show images, depending on the needs of your students and your academic goals.

Teaching Language and Content Together

Instruction of ELs often involves teaching content and language together. This can be challenging, given the lack of resources for content instruction that also include support for teaching language. And yet, teachers are required to do both.

Researchers have shown that context is an important factor in learning academic language. Many scholars agree that listening activities within the context of a content area is a more efficient way to promote second language acquisition. Complex texts and stories have more complex words. In addition to learning about the world, listening is an excellent way for students to build content knowledge.[14]

The integration of content and language in teaching is one of the four "big ideas" underlying the updated 2020 WIDA framework. The update makes this connection explicit and specific. WIDA says that "multilingual learners develop content and language concurrently, with academic content as a context for language learning and language as a means for learning academic content."[15] And it encourages teachers to use multiple means of communication including speaking, images, charts, gestures, and other means.

In many countries outside of the United States, students are required to learn English as a part of the K–12 curriculum. For that reason, many of the studies on how best to learn English are conducted in other countries, not in the US K–12 classroom. In Europe, teachers have integrated language skills with content in a practice called content-based teaching or CBT. According to researchers Wesche and Skehan, there are two types of CBT. In the "strong" approach, the primary goal is to learn content, with the secondary goal of becoming fluent in the language. The "weaker" approach focuses on communicative fluency in the target language using a content-based curriculum.[16] The instructions on Listenwise would be considered the "strong" approach to CBT, as they are meant to be used by both language teachers and general education teachers.

Because of the growing population of English learners, it's necessary to teach both content and language. But it's also been shown to increase motivation and engagement when language is connected to content. A study of elementary school students in Taiwan found that "teaching listening skills could be integrated into the content-based course, and certain listening skills were greatly improved." The study concluded that "explicit instruction in listening skills, when accompanied by interactive tasks in a content-based language learning program" can improve English instruction.[17] Podcasts are a perfect vehicle for this type of teaching because they naturally integrate language and content.

DURING LISTENING

In this section, students are expected to do these activities while listening to the podcast. This can be done either synchronously or asynchronously. Students can be listening individually with headphones in a remote or blended setting, or you can play the story out loud over the speakers in your classroom. If teaching synchronously, you may want to project the interactive transcript onto a screen for everyone to see.

Scaffolding Instruction for Listening

- Audio transcripts, slower speed, and close listening
- Listening organizers (language identification)

Listening with no support is difficult, especially to any recorded audio, such as a podcast. In a conversation there are often facial and gesture cues. Without visual cues, without a transcript to follow, without knowledge of the topic or a preview of the vocabulary, listening to a story about an academic topic is hard.

Have you ever been to a foreign country and thought, "If they just spoke really slowly I might be able to understand them"? Listening to someone speak in their native tongue at a regular pace is difficult, even if you have years of training and practice in that foreign language. It's also exhausting. It takes a lot of energy to focus intently on a speaker, whether they are in front of you or on the TV, radio, or the internet. If your attention wanders for a split second, you could be lost for the rest of the conversation or presentation. And if you don't know one critical vocabulary word that connects all the concepts together, you could be completely lost! But the opposite is also true. If you know one word, you might use context, background knowledge, or context to fill in the blanks. Breaking down listening into smaller, slower chunks helps.

AUDIO TRANSCRIPT

As I explored in the chapter on listening and reading, reading the transcript while listening supports comprehension. This is even more true and important for ELs.

Every podcast on Listenwise has an interactive transcript. It progresses in sync with the audio and highlights the words as they are read. The transcript allows students to follow along, stop and hear a word again, and see the spelling of words as they are read authentically. The transcript can also be downloaded and printed for students. As seen in Figure 6.1, an example of an interactive transcript on Listenwise, the words are highlighted in blue as they are spoken in the audio.

Because the podcasts contain authentic spoken language with many different voices, pacing, and cultural backgrounds, students can be well supported by reading along while listening.

A study of the reading application SiMBi found that the reading while listening app, which pairs picture books with authentically read audio, "is a promising tool to potentially improve both reading comprehension and fluency of the English language."[18]

Figure 6.1 Example of an interactive transcript on Listenwise.

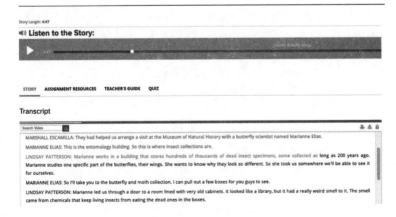

> *I'm impressed by the ELL supports on the Listen-*
> *wise site. They have high interest materials that*
> *students can access and listen to with the ability*
> *to follow along with the transcript that highlights*
> *words as they are read. This helps my English*
> *learners at all levels of language proficiency.*
> —Sam Perez, Lowell Scott middle school ESOL
> teacher, Boise, ID

SLOWED AUDIO

Speech rate is a major part of listening comprehension in any language. But there is controversy over what speech rate is best for language learners.[19] There is agreement, however, that slowing down the rate of speech gives students time to process the information. When you are teaching a concept and alter your speech rate to make sure that the English learners in your class understand you, you run the risk of losing the native speakers who will tune out. Using podcasts is an excellent way to adjust the rate of speech as needed for each student. Software now makes it easy to adjust speech rate. You've probably seen the feature on your podcast app. You can choose to listen to an episode at .5×, 1.5×, or 2×.

On Listenwise, there is a simple button to toggle between regular and slowed audio. The slower version is 20% slower than the normal speech rate. The transcript stays synchronized to the audio at the slower rate. That way, students can still follow the transcript while listening at a slower rate of speech, which can help them catch more complex concepts and ideas. Slowing down the audio can serve both language development and content understanding.

> *I love the ability to slow down the content, because*
> *it makes it easier to understand but still authen-*
> *tic. And it doesn't allow students to skim through*
> *the podcast.*
> —Laura Rosenfeld, 11th-grade teacher,
> Boston, MA

CLOSE LISTENING

Similar to close reading, using close listening protocols can greatly improve comprehension. Such activities require listening to the audio several times for different purposes. While you can prepare this yourself with any audio, I've shared the following example using an NPR story.

Class Activity: Close Listening Guide

The purpose of the first listen in the close listening exercise is to check for understanding and activate prior knowledge. The second close listen focuses on a language element of the story, in this case modal auxiliary verbs. After the third listen, students are asked to summarize the story and discuss the main idea.

Middle/High School Students: Use the story "Charles Dickens—The Jon Stewart of His Day?" about Dickens's writing. [8]

First Listen

Stop at 0:34. What do you think the radio host means when she describes the Lowell mills as "model factories"? What might a model factory look like?

Stop at 1:01. At this point in history, which would have been better to work at, a mill in Lowell, or an English factory?

Stop at 1:47. Make sure students are familiar with the terms "cellar" and "basement" and understand what the speaker means by "raw sewage seeping through the walls."

Stop at 2:47. What is the radio host implying when she suggests that maybe Dickens saw some sort of "spirit" in the Lowell Mills girls?

Stop at 3:16. Why was Dickens opposed to unions if he cared about the conditions of workers?

Stop at 4:32. How did Dickens' travels to the United States affect his writing and his attitude towards his work?

Second Listen

Listen a second time to focus on the modal auxiliary verbs could, would, should, and ought. Review that modal auxiliaries are verbs that are used along with other verbs to slightly change their meaning. These types of verbs can also be used in "If . . . then . . ." statements to make express cause and effect relationships.

Stop at 1:26. What could sometimes get caught in mill machinery?

Stop at 2:52. What would Dickens have been displeased to see in the Lowell Mills girls?

Stop at 3:07. What did Dickens think ought to be seen in society and in mill owners?

Stop at 4:18. How did going abroad give Dickens the hope that the social problems he saw in the factories could be solved?

Third Listen

Listen a third time to summarize the audio story and identify the main idea.

The audio and a full lesson called "Charles Dickens Reflects on Society" can be accessed at https//:listenwise.com/book.

Listening Organizers

Good listeners often take notes. Providing listening organizers to students to support their note taking and use of metacognitive strategies while listening can be very helpful. The organizers can focus on vocabulary, grammar, sentence structure, and other language skills, or they can focus on key ideas. They can serve as note-taking guides so that students aren't starting with a blank page (or blank computer screen) when asked to write down important information from a story. Teachers can provide a structure for the note-taking that allows students to fill in key information when they hear it. This could be a simple T-chart graphic organizer or a Fact-Question-Response organizer.

This note-taking strategy, called "guided notes," has been shown to substantially increase student achievement, according to research across grade levels.[20]

Class Activity: Guided Note-Taking

Encouraging students to use metacognitive skills while listening is an excellent way to improve comprehension. This can be done by following along with the transcript while listening, or tracking phrases as they appear in the story using the "Language Identification Organizer" on Listenwise. It is a sequential list of phrases, which can help students find their way back into a story if they lose track while listening.

Elementary School Students: Use the Tumble podcast called "Journey to the Center of the Earth." [9] Create an organizer with three columns: Fact, Question, and Response. Students will use the worksheet to keep track of their thoughts as they listen to the audio story. In the "Fact" column, record interesting or useful factual information about the topic. In the "Question" column, write questions that occur as they listen. Finally, in the "Response" column, make a list of responses to the story. Add the clarification that a response could be: an answer to a question you had; a reaction you had to something you heard with examples based on categories of: (1) What surprised you? (2) What confirmed something you already knew? (3) What was something confusing you heard? (4) What's something that made you think differently? (5) What's something you found hard to believe?

Middle/High School Students: Use the NPR story "For New Immigrants To The U.S., Ellis Island Still Means A Lot" about Ellis Island. [10] You will guide your students to make a simple T-chart by drawing a line across the top of a page and one down the middle. They should label the left column Facts About Past Immigration and the right column Facts About Current Immigration. As they listen, take notes in the two columns to guide their listening.

The audio and a printable PDF of the graphic organizers can also be found on https://listenwise.com/book and by searching for the lessons "The Center of the Earth" and "New Immigrants and Ellis Island Today."

AFTER LISTENING

In this section, we'll review activities that help students demonstrate their understanding by speaking. You may want to hold speaking practice based on listening when you are having synchronous instruction, either live in the classroom or online. Students can be paired up for a discussion or they could record themselves.

Encouraging Speaking Practice to Deepen Listening Comprehension

Listening is "good preparation for conversation," says Zwiers of Stanford University. Conversations happen in real time, and the more learners can quickly understand authentic spoken language and respond, the more fluent they become. In a live conversation, students need to feel confident enough to stop the speaker and ask for clarification. But with recorded audio, you have the ability to chunk it. You can stop the audio after a complex idea is introduced and ask students: What do you think the speaker means by that?

Zwiers told me in an interview that listening helps ELs produce clear spoken language. Not only do you learn a lot of words, but you learn grammatical structures, which are an important part of learning how to speak.

Listening is hard work for multilingual learners. They will be asking themselves, why am I listening? Building listening comprehension habits won't be enough. You should state a clear purpose for listening and process the listening orally and build on ideas.

A listener's response is also a key feature of effective listening. Can students demonstrate what they learned by speaking to the class or in small groups? Can they use the academic language they heard in a story in another context? One way to foster conversation is to select a story that lends itself to debate. When an issue is presented in such a way that it offers multiple dimensions or perspectives, it allows students to engage more easily in conversation. According to Zwiers, deliberate speaking "cultivates such thinking skills as evaluating, comparing, inferring cause and effect, and persuading, along with the language of those skills."[21]

Class Activity: Stronger and Clearer Each Time[22]

This activity is essentially three think/pair/shares in a row. In a typical think/pair/share, students are asked to think individually about what they heard and then share it with their partners. In this activity, you add multiple pairs and shares so that students can borrow and build on each others' ideas and practice their answers multiple times.

In this activity, you should explain that borrowing the ideas and the vocabulary and grammar of others is okay because you are building a stronger and clearer understanding each time.

For example, you can use NPR's story "Report: More Than Half of U.S. Children Now Own a Smartphone By Age 11." [11]

Students might share their opinions about why kids in the United States are getting smartphones at a younger and younger age. They can also ask the following questions:

What are parents' roles in determining how smartphones are used by children?

Why would young kids need cell phones?

What were the different behaviors between boys' and girls' media use in the study?

What were the differences between how Black and Hispanic teens use media?

What was the most surprising finding from the study?

All of these questions can provoke thoughtful discussion and help students use some of the academic vocabulary words in the story: comparable, commonality, differ, socialize, and ethnic.

(*Source:* Jeff Zwiers, Stanford University, for inspiration for this activity)

LISTENING IS THE EQUALIZER

I believe listening can be an equalizer in learning. What do I mean by this? The approaches I've shared about using podcasts to teach language and content can benefit both ELs and native English speakers. Listening to high quality audio stories is beneficial to everyone. For ELs, building the scaffolding of vocabulary and background knowledge sets them up for listening success. For English speakers, less scaffolding may be required, but they will still be engaged, learning content, and building academic vocabulary and background knowledge.

What I love about using podcasts is that everyone is listening to the same authentically spoken story with the exact same language and content. The stories evoke anticipation, emotion, and other elements that tap into shared human experiences. Listening to stories enables the English learner to be carried along by the real-world emotion of the stories, without getting stuck on a word they might not understand. Unlike reading programs that downshift the reading level for students, all students are hearing the same vocabulary and sentence structure. And listening to the expression and tone can help students understand meaning and be engaged, which are critical motivators for language learning. This is the intent of differentiated instruction—providing extra instructional support where needed for learners to access the same curriculum content.

I see now that the factors that supported my success and the challenges I faced as a language learner are similar to those experienced by thousands of ELs in our classrooms. For me, I had the choice to learn a language, which contributed to me dedicating myself to it. For many ELs in our schools, it's not a choice, but a necessity. Think of the situational factors of your students to understand where they are coming from. The input I had to learn Swahili and Portuguese (once I moved to Brazil) were authentic. I was actively working to understand the language.

My processing strategies were multisensory and made the language stick. In Kenya, I learned to cook Swahili dishes while speaking with my teachers. In Brazil, I practiced every morning ordering the same breakfast at the local bakery. I listened closely to how the server repeated my order, so that I could imitate it the next time. Looking back now, I see how these were research-proven strategies to learn a language. It's difficult to bring this level of authenticity to a classroom of English learners. My belief is that listening to authentically spoken English in the context of engaging narratives can help.

REFLECTION AND PLANNING

Take this opportunity to write some reflections and plans for action.

Do you speak another language? What factors affected your language learning (TV, cooking, music, etc.)? What can you apply from your successes and challenges that might be relevant to your students?

_____

_____

Experiment with your speech rate. Try different speaking rates with your students to see if you can find a pace that helps your English learners without alienating your native speakers.

_____

What is your content-based approach (CBT) to teaching? Strong or weak? How can you employ listening activities to enhance your content teaching?

_____

How will you use listening to equalize the learning opportunities available to your students?

_____

_____

Audio Resources

[1] Feifer, Gregory. (2007, November 7). Glossy view of the Soviet era takes hold in Russia. NPR, www.npr.org/templates/story/story.php?storyId=15881559.

[2] Martin, Rachel. (2020, July 20). "Dog Has a Fondness for the Porch at Family's Previous Residence." NPR, www.npr.org/2020/07/20/892943721/dog-has-a-fondness-for-the-porch-at-familys-previous-residence.

[3] Ulaby, Neda. (2014, August 16). Lois Lowry says "The Giver" was inspired by her father's memory loss. NPR, www.npr.org/2014/08/16/340170478/lois-lowry-says-the-giver-was-inspired-by-her-fathers-memory-loss.

[4] Inskeep, Steve. (2020, September 11). Alligator pool floatie surprises Florida couple. NPR, www.npr.org/2020/09/11/911828391/alligator-pool-floatie-surprises-florida-couple.

[5] Naylor, Brian. (2011, September 11). Homeland security remains an agency in progress. NPR, www.npr.org/2011/09/11/140367706/homeland-security-remains-an-agency-in-progress.

[6] Felde, Kitty. (2018, August 29). Episode 73—Tuck Everlasting by Natalie Babbitt. *Book Club for Kids*, www.bookclubforkids.org/new-blog/2018/8/27/episode-73-tuck-everlasting-by-natalie-babbitt.

[7] Montagne, Renee. (2004, September 20). Toni Morrison's "Good" Ghosts. NPR, www.npr.org/2004/09/20/3912464/toni-morrisons-good-ghosts.

[8] Young, Robin. (2012, February 3). Charles Dickens—The Jon Stewart of his day? *Charles Dickens—The Jon Stewart of His Day? | Here & Now*, WBUR, www.wbur.org/hereandnow/2012/02/03/charles-dickens-anniversary.

[9] Patterson, Lindsay, & Marshall Escamilla. (2017, January 13). Journey to the center of the Earth with Ta-Shana Taylor. *Tumblepodcast*, www.sciencepodcastforkids.com/single-post/2017/01/13/journey-to-the-center-of-the-earth-with-ta-shana-taylor.

[10] Wang, Hansi Lo. (2015, May 20). For New Immigrants To The U.S., Ellis Island Still Means A Lot. NPR, www.npr.org/sections/codeswitch/2015/05/20/408157318/recent-immigrants-find-ellis-island-still-relevant.

[11] Kamenetz, Anya. (2019, October 29). Report: More than half of U.S. children now own a smartphone by age 11. NPR, www.npr.org/2019/10/29/774306250/report-more-than-half-of-u-s-children-now-own-a-smartphone-by-age-11.

References

1. National Center for Education Statistics. (2020, May). *English language learners in public schools*. https://nces.ed.gov/programs/coe/indicator_cgf.asp.

2. National Education Association. (2020, July). *English language learners*. https://www.nea.org/resource-library/english-language-learners.

3. Hunsaker, R. (1983). *Listening and speaking*. Englewood, CO: Morton.

4. Roussel, S., Gruson, B., & Galan, J-P. (2019). What types of training improve learners' performances in second language listening comprehension? *International Journal of Listening* 33(1), 39–52, https://www.tandfonline.com/doi/citedby/10.1080/10904018.2017.1331133?scroll=top&need=true.

5. English Language Development Standards. (n.d.). https://wida.wisc.edu/teach/standards/eld (accessed September 12, 2020).

6. Colorin Colorado. (2013, November 12). Vocabulary development with ELLs. https://www.readingrockets.org/article/vocabulary-development-ells (accessed September 4, 2020).

7. Murphey, D., PhD. (2014, December). The academic achievement of English language learners: Data for the U.S. and each of the states. https://www.childtrends.org/wp-content/uploads/2015/07/2014-62AcademicAchieve-mentEnglish.pdf (accessed September 4, 2020).

8. Hakuta, K., Butler, Y.G., & Witt, D. (2000). *How long does it take English learners to attain proficiency?* (pp. 1–30, Rep.). Stanford, CA: University of California Linguistic Minority Research Institute.

9. Dickinson, D.K., & Neuman, S. (2003). *Handbook of early literacy research.* New York, NY: Guilford Press.

10. Miller, M., & Veatch, N. (2011). *Literacy in context (LinC): Choosing instructional strategies to teach reading in content areas for students grades 5–12.* New York, NY: Pearson.

11. Madani, B.S., & Kheirzadeh, S. (2018). The impact of pre-listening activities on EFL learners; Listening comprehension. *International Journal of Listening.* doi: 10.1080/10904 018.2018.1523679.

12. Beck, I.L., McKeown, M.G., & Kucan, L. (2013). *Bringing words to life: Robust vocabulary instruction,* second edition. New York, NY: Guilford.

13. Zwiers, J. (2014). Facilitating whole-class discussions for content and language development. In *Building academic language: Meeting common core standards across disciplines, grades 5–12* (2nd ed., pp. 133–134). San Francisco, CA: Jossey-Bass.

14. Bedjou, A. (2006). Using radio programs in the EFL classroom. *English Teaching Forum, 44*(1), 28–31.

15. Wisconsin Center for Education Research. (2020). WIDA English language development standards framework, 2020 edition kindergarten–grade 12, pp. 19–20.

16. Wesche, M.B., & Skehan, P. (2002). Communicative, task-based, and content-based language instruction. In R.B. Kaplan (Ed.), *The Oxford handbook of applied linguistics* (pp. 207–228). Oxford, UK: Oxford University Press.

17. Chou, M. (2013). A content-based approach to teaching and testing listening skills to grade 5 EFL learners. *International Journal of Listening, 27*(3), 172–185, doi: 10.1080/10 904018.2013.822270.

18. Friedland, A., Gilman, M., Johnson, M., & Ambaye, A.D. (2017). Does reading-while-listening enhance students' reading fluency? Preliminary results from school experiments in rural Uganda. *Journal of Education and Practice, 8*, 82–95.

19. Zhao, Y. (1997, March). Effects of listeners' control of speech rate on second language comprehension. *Applied Linguistics, 18*(1), 49–68, https://doi.org/10.1093/applin/18.1.49.

20. Haydon, T., Mancil, R., Kroeger, S., McLeskey, J., & Wan-Yu, J.L. (2011). A review of the effectiveness of guided notes for students who struggle learning academic content. *Preventing School Failure: Alternative Education for Children and Youth, 55.* 226–231. doi:10.1080/10459 88X.2010.548415.

21. Zwiers, J. (2014). Facilitating whole-class discussions for content and language development. In *Building academic language: Meeting Common Core standards across disciplines, grades 5–12* (2nd ed., p. 154). San Francisco, CA: Jossey-Bass.

22. Zwiers, J. (2020). *Authentic speaking & listening*, www.jeffzwiers.org/speaking-listening.

Chapter 7

Assessing Listening

Vicki Beck knows who will volunteer when she asks students to read a passage out loud. They are the same kids she knows have mastered reading. And when she asks students to repeat back what they heard her say, they are usually the same kids.

She worries more about the students who are silent. It might just mean they weren't paying attention to what she said, not that they didn't understand it. But how can she tell the difference? Maybe they don't have good listening comprehension skills.

What frustrates her is there are so many ways to test her students' reading and math abilities, but not their listening skills. Vicki has been told by parents and supervisors she is a good listener. And she knows that listening as an interpersonal skill is important, but good listening skills are also vitally important to academic learning. And for her, knowing which students need more support is critical.

Vicki wishes there was a practical way to assess listening, as there is for other key skills. That would allow her to quickly check her students' listening skills without having to question each *one individually after they listen to a podcast, which time does not allow.*

STANDARDIZING LISTENING TESTS

Until very recently, there has been no practical way to evaluate students' listening comprehension skills. This is a huge problem, considering how much of what we learn is learned through listening. Let's contrast this situation with reading. There are a plethora of reading tests available for teachers to use, which fill all kinds of needs.

The following table shows the kinds of reading assessments available. Most students will take **formative** reading tests, **interim** reading tests, and a **summative** reading test, all during the course of each school year.

Types of Reading Tests

	Formative tests	Interim tests	Summative tests
What are they?	These are questions and tasks that usually occur during classroom instruction. Teachers use these tests to evaluate students' understanding of the lesson content. They can also diagnose gaps	These tests reveal students' current achievement levels. For example, how well has a student mastered the grade-level state standards that they are supposed to have mastered by this time in	These are longer, comprehensive tests that assess students on a complete set of standards, often for a whole school year. They evaluate students against standards, but also evaluate the

	Formative tests	Interim tests	Summative tests
	in students' skills. This helps teachers decide next steps in instruction. Feedback on these tests is usually immediate or very rapid.	the year? They show what students know now, and what they are ready to learn. They may also show a student's learning trajectory, or rate of growth.	effectiveness of the educational environment. Information about students' individual strengths or weaknesses is limited.
Who or what is assessed?	Individual students	Individual students and classes	The educational environment: students, teachers, curriculum, school systems, etc.
How often does it happen?	Ongoing, such as every week.	Intermittent, such as three times a year.	Once a year, usually the end of the year.

Needless to say, teachers can get a lot of information about students' reading skills. While some states use a standardized listening test that's wrapped into the English Language Arts (ELA) portion of a summative test, for the most part there are few formative or interim listening tests. In other words, all the things we know about students' reading skills are *not known* about their listening skills. There are multiple ways teachers consider where students are in their listening comprehension and assess it in class. But at the moment, we cannot independently verify that students understand the content of what they listen to, we cannot diagnose deficiencies in their listening skills, we cannot compare their listening skills to their reading skills, and we cannot ascertain whether their listening skills are "on grade level" compared to their peers or whether their listening skills are developing at a normal rate.

Well, that is, until now. In a little while, we will discuss how these things are now possible with Listenwise and the Lexile Framework for Listening. But first, let's talk a bit more about these "standards" mentioned in the earlier table.

Students are often asked to take tests so that their skills and knowledge can be evaluated against standards, such as state standards or the Common Core standards. The Common Core includes learning goals for listening and speaking in the ELA standards. For example, here is one for fifth grade:

Pose and respond to specific questions by making comments that contribute to the discussion and elaborate on the remarks of others.

Like many of the standards, this one involves discussion and relates to communication and collaboration. This can be assessed as part of a classroom activity, but it would be very challenging to assess this as part of a large-scale, standardized assessment, such as an interim or summative test. It also involves listening and talking, and so does not disambiguate a student's listening comprehension skills from their overall communication skills. Here is another standard:

Summarize the points a speaker makes and explain how each claim is supported by reasons and evidence.

This one involves listening, analyzing, and summarizing. It is actually very similar to reading standards, except that instead of reading a text, the student is listening to a speaker. But this kind of summary activity presumably means that the student has to not only listen, but also speak or write. And, it would consume a lot of test time. This learning goal is difficult to assess in a standardized test, where there are time constraints and the marking of the students' work has to be fair.

When it comes to listening skills, many state standards and Common Core standards are clear about articulating the kind of behaviors we want our students to be good at—such as communication, collaboration, and critical thinking. But, when it comes to making test questions that assess these standards, they are logistically difficult to administer, time consuming, and challenging to score in a way that is fair and objective.

For these reasons, many states simply do not assess listening (or speaking) in their end-of-year exams, even if these skills are included in part of their standards. As of 2020, approximately 40 states use the Common Core standards, but only 22 states test listening on their summative exams. Twelve of those states use the Smarter Balance Assessment Consortium (SBAC) test, while others use an adapted version. Indiana uses the ILEARN assessment and Florida uses the Florida Standards Assessment or FSA.

Listening tends to be assessed in grades 3–8. But this varies: Florida continues to test listening yearly until the 10th grade, and in California listening is tested in grades 3–8 and again in the 11th grade. In an analysis by Listenwise, more than 10 million students are tested on listening comprehension skills every year. That's less than one-fifth of all U.S. K–12 students.

But even in these 22 states that do test listening, it is usually a minor part of the ELA exam. On the SBAC, a typical listening question has students listening to audio that is less than two minutes in length and answering three or four questions. They are not given the text in print but are allowed to listen multiple times. Since SBAC assesses one of the Common Core standards that refers to "written text read aloud," many of the audio passages do not exhibit the natural expressiveness of everyday speech. Rather, the test questions assess comprehension of text via the medium of audio rather than the medium of printed text. All this has the effect of including listening in the exam and "checking off" that the standard has been assessed, without really doing enough testing of listening skills to be able to say much about students' listening comprehension ability.

TESTING LISTENING WITH ELs

There is, however, one kind of test that involves listening and is widespread in the United States—tests for English language learners, or ELs. These are tests such as the ELPAC in California, the TELPAS in Texas, and the ACCESS test by WIDA, which is used in 40 states that have smaller populations of EL students. These tests typically view the four skills with equal importance—reading, writing, speaking, and listening—and so the assessment of listening is given a similar amount of test time and weighting as reading. Often, the standards for ELs are more concrete and easier to make into test questions. As an example, the WIDA test has performance indicators as part of the standards, which can be more easily applied to standardized assessment. Figure 7.1 shows WIDA standards that link to Common Core third-grade math standards, concerning measuring the length of objects.

Similarly, Figure 7.2 shows WIDA standards that link to Common Core eighth-grade standards for analyzing universal themes of literature.

As you can see, these EL exams have woven listening skills into their standards and into the tasks that students perform in the exam. As many as 5 million students across the United States take EL exams every year, and both interim and summative tests are available. But for mainstream, non-EL students, options for such a rigorous listening assessment are limited. Up until 2015, testing listening was almost entirely subjective. At that time, a Listenwise analysis of approximately 15 standardized listening

Figure 7.1 WIDA standards for third-grade math.
Source: WIDA.

	Level 1 Entering	Level 2 Emerging	Level 3 Developing	Level 4 Expanding	Level 5 Bridging	
					Level 6—Reaching	
LISTENING	Follow oral instructions to identify lengths of objects following a model with a partner	Follow oral instructions to categorize objects according to their length following a model with a partner	Follow oral instructions to order objects according to their lengths following a model with a partner	Follow oral instructions to compare the lengths of objects using a template with a partner	Follow multi-step oral instructions to compare the lenghts of objects with a partner	

Figure 7.2 WIDA standards for eighth-grade ELA analyzing universal themes of literature.
Source: WIDA.

	Level 1 Entering	Level 2 Emerging	Level 3 Developing	Level 4 Expanding	Level 5 Bridging	
						Level 6—Reaching
LISTENING	Select illustrations depicting literary characters, themes, and plots based on oral statements using environmental print (e.g., posters about character types and themes)	Select illustrations depicting literary characters, themes, and plots based on oral descriptions using environmental print	Classify examples of literary characters, themes, and plots based on oral descriptions with a partner	Find patterns related to literary characters, themes, and plots using graphic organizers with a partner	Predict evolution of literary characters, themes, and plots	

comprehension tests found that none tested all aspects of listening, and none of them were fully administered online. Typical practice for testing listening in the classroom was almost entirely paper and pen, highly variable, and used a random selection of text. For example, the Stanford 10 exam used to address listening comprehension by testing only vocabulary. While much of the exam was online, it required teachers to dictate a vocabulary passage aloud and ask questions that students answered online. This was prone to errors and lacked standardized administration. These constraints have held back our understanding of the importance of listening and the role it plays in reading and learning.

CREATING FORMATIVE LISTENING TESTS

With listening skills increasingly appearing in widely used standards and on many state exams, there is a need to start practicing listening more in the classroom. However, until recently there were no tests for practicing listening in the classroom. There are ways to try and check for listening comprehension. Some teachers use checklists when listening to students in a class discussion, or have students take notes and write about other student's speeches. But such tools may not be reliable and could introduce bias.

Listenwise created the first ever formative online receptive multiple-choice test of listening comprehension with a progress monitoring dashboard. It is an assessment that is standardized in its administration online, more comprehensive, and less subjective than previous testing methods. Listenwise developed the listening assessment in 2017, working with experts in the reading field, and the few experts in the listening and reading field, such as Dr. Tiffany Hogan, to decide on the key listening comprehension skills. The goal was to find a way to measure listening passages and use the quizzes to track student progress.

Educator's Story: Building Students' Listening Profiles

I am a high school History teacher in California and I've used Listenwise to improve my students' listening skills. After assigning 10–15 stories with quizzes each semester, I realized that I had created detailed listening profiles on each student. I began asking students to reflect on the skill they were having trouble answering correctly. This helped students see where they need to improve. I also like that students can see the progress they've made over time on Listenwise quizzes.

I used the Listenwise Literacy Coach's Guide to create additional activities and watched quiz scores improve until almost all students scored 100% regularly. I work with gifted students, so they were motivated to do well. But using the quizzes helped my students realize that listening is a skill they can control. One student told me that they know if they pay attention better to the story, they can score well.

California is an SBAC state, so listening skills are tested on the high stakes test called the CAASP. Practicing with quizzes that are modeled after the SBAC prepares my students really well for the high stakes test.

Since then, I have used longer audio lectures to improve their note-taking skills and listening stamina. Recently, Listenwise has rolled out Lexile® Audio Measures and improved their data reporting. These are great steps forward, because once students learn that active listening is under their power, there is no stopping them. Good listeners become great communicators. Listenwise has helped me and my students understand that it is possible to develop listening skills.

—Scott M. Petri, high school History
teacher, Valencia, California

To make the quizzes the Listenwise team identified elements that are included in reading assessments because of the important connection between reading and listening.[1] While listening and reading both require comprehension skills, many of which overlap, the application of those skills can vary somewhat across contexts. For example, students need to practice identifying and summarizing the most important ideas in audio stories, which can be organized differently than print stories. The kinds of natural speech found in these audio stories typically does not follow the structure of a written article with a clearly articulated lead and a linear progression of ideas. When students are listening to a speaker's voice, they can also pay attention to the tone, emphasis, and pacing of the speech, in other words prosody, to make inferences and identify the speaker's point of view.

Eight Key Listening Comprehension Skills Assessed through Listenwise Quizzes

1. **Recognizing Literal Meaning:** Questions about facts, details, or information explicitly stated in the audio story
2. **Understanding Vocabulary:** Questions about the meanings of words as they are used in the context of the audio story
3. **Making Inferences:** Questions asking students to make inferences as they listen to audio stories,

interpreting what is said by going beyond the literal meaning

4. **Identifying Main Idea:** Questions asking students to identify the central idea or gist of an audio story

5. **Determining Purpose:** Questions asking students to determine the purpose of an audio story

6. **Analyzing Reasoning:** Questions asking students to analyze reasoning supporting a claim in an audio story

7. **Drawing Conclusions:** Questions asking students to draw conclusions by synthesizing information in an audio story

8. **Finding Evidence:** Questions asking students to identify statements or details in an audio story that provide evidence to support claims or conclusions

Every quiz tests the first four skills: recognizing literal meaning, understanding vocabulary, making inferences, and identifying main idea. In some cases, an additional fifth or sixth question assesses higher order skills.

Figure 7.3 Listenwise's eight strands of listening comprehension skills.
Source: Listenwise.

Listening Comprehension Skills

RECOGNIZING LITERAL MEANING   UNDERSTANDING VOCABULARY   MAKING INFERENCES   IDENTIFYING MAIN IDEA

DETERMINING PURPOSE   ANALYZING REASONING   DRAWING CONCLUSIONS   FINDING EVIDENCE

Figure 7.4 Sample quiz question assessing literal meaning.
Source: Listenwise.

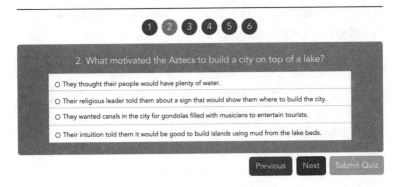

For example, Figure 7.4 is a question that assesses the skill of Recognizing Literal Meaning.

The quizzes are autoscored, giving both students and teachers immediate feedback. Students can see what questions they got wrong and the correct answer. And teachers can see on their dashboard, shown in Figure 7.5, how students perform across listening skills.

Figure 7.5 Example of a class summary quiz report on the Listenwise teacher dashboard.
Source: Listenwise.

Class Quiz Average: **60%**

Students	Total Correct	Literal	Vocabulary	Main Idea	Inference
		1st Period ELA			
Overall	60% 14 of 18	78% 14 of 18	78% 14 of 18	39% 7 of 18	56% 10 of 18
Daniel Brady	60% 	100% 2 of 2	50% 1 of 2	50% 1 of 2	50% 1 of 2
Emma Coleman	55% 	100% 2 of 2	100% 2 of 2	50% 1 of 2	50% 1 of 2
Julius Dodson	73% 	50% 1 of 2	100% 2 of 2	100% 2 of 2	50% 1 of 2
Lauren Gonsalves	27% 	50% 1 of 2	50% 1 of 2	0% 0 of 2	0% 0 of 2

While other digital tools such as Newsela, Reading A-Z, and Readworks have created similar formative reading tests, Listenwise was the first company to create this kind of practice listening test for U.S. schools.

> *After using listening quizzes, my students showed great improvement in the area of listening on their state assessment. In fact, listening comprehension was one of their greatest areas of strength on the assessment.*
>
> —Kate Waggoner, middle school teacher, Winston, OR

When breaking new ground, it was difficult to find experienced item writers. Listenwise worked with a highly regarded reading consultant who trained and hired item writers to create the listening quizzes. But from the beginning, something wasn't right.

In the early days, after a quiz was in draft form, our team would take the listening quizzes to review them. I noticed there wasn't agreement about the main idea of a story. Because these quizzes were on NPR news stories or podcasts, they were longer than the typical SBAC exam audio passage and sometimes covered several themes. But there was something wrong in the way the main idea answers were conveyed in the early test answers.

The Listenwise team had a call with our consultant to figure out the problem. The consultant walked us through the item-writing process. She said a writer would receive the story and the transcript, read the transcript, and write the items. "When do they listen to the story?" I asked. It turned out they were not listening to the story. They were writing the items based entirely on reading the transcript.

This made sense to the writers because they were skilled item writers for reading passages. But the difference this made in writing a question about the main idea for a listening quiz was significant. It proved what I already knew to be true from decades of reporting for NPR—listening to someone's voice, intonation, emotion, and emphasis is different than reading. Listening can convey the same basic material. For instance, the writers never made mistakes on questions about vocabulary or literal meaning. But the overall listening experience, the way you hear a story, can better convey the main idea than reading the transcript. The problem was easy to correct. The item writers were told to first *listen* to the story without reading the transcript and write the main idea question. While these formative listening assessments were welcomed by teachers using Listenwise, it wasn't enough to accurately track student's progress and achieve the bigger literacy goal—improve reading through listening.

Theory of Impact

Our determination to build a listening assessment tool was built on a theory of change developed by Dr. Hogan. Despite the long-standing recognition that a variety of language skills are inherently important to (and significant precursors of) skilled reading comprehension (e.g., Gough & Tunmer, 1986), researchers and educators have failed to leverage this relationship in the design of comprehensive listening assessments for children; rather, the literature to date largely consists of applied studies targeting only one or perhaps two skill areas (e.g., vocabulary). But teachers want and need valid and authentic measures of listening comprehension that yield data to drive instruction and inform differentiation of instruction for learners at all levels.

As shown in Figure 7.6, we theorize that implementation of quality listening experiences will result in increases in the quantity and quality of language-based listening instruction within classrooms. As Figure 7.5 also indicates, we theorize that changes in teachers' instructional practices, including use of assessment data to inform instruction, will lead to changes in children's language and literacy skills. These include proximal changes in children's language skills and listening comprehension and distal changes in reading comprehension and lifelong literacy.

Figure 7.6   Theory of Impact.
Source: Adapted from Dr. Tiffany Hogan's Theory of Change.

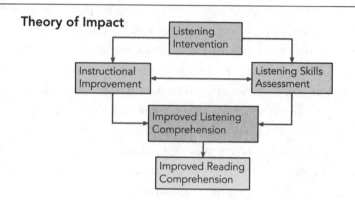

As this Theory of Impact makes clear, the potential for children's listening and reading comprehension to improve hinges on teachers' access to and implementation of quality, evidence-based listening materials and assessments within their classrooms. In essence, more availability of higher-quality listening materials will result in improved learning outcomes.

DEVELOPING A LISTENING SCALE

This all represents good progress in assessing listening, because with the Listenwise assessments, teachers can now ascertain which skills are proving difficult for students and adjust instruction accordingly. But, several challenges still remained. Remember all the things we can assess with reading, that we cannot do with listening? They include (1) checking whether students' listening skills are on grade level; (2) measuring whether listening skills are developing at a normal rate; (3) matching students to material that is appropriate for their level. And, we can add to that (4) comparing students' listening skills to their reading skills. Happily, all of these were resolved by the introduction of the Lexile Framework for Listening.

In order to overcome these challenges, it is necessary to have a scale on which we can track students' developmental listening skills. For example, students with lower or emerging comprehension skills score lower on the numerical scale, and students with higher or proficient skills score higher on the scale.

Let's take a couple of reading scales as an example. Two of the most widely used scales are the Fountas & Pinnell Classroom™ Guided Reading Collection and the Lexile Framework for Reading. The Fountas & Pinnell Classroom™ Guided Reading Collection has hundreds of books that span text levels on a scale of A to Z. It's meant for small group instruction. Students progress from very simple books (level A) to more complex books (level Z). Teachers can periodically assess where students are on the scale and move students to the next level when they are ready. The Fountas and Pinnell approach to reading assessment is subjective, because books are evaluated by reading specialists and assigned a letter, and teachers evaluate students to find books that are suitable for them.

The Lexile Framework for Reading uses a more scientific approach. A student's level of reading comprehension is assessed on a test, usually with multiple choice or cloze (i.e., fill in the blank) test questions. Then, they are assigned a Lexile student measure on a scale from 0L to 2,000L, although foundational reading skills continue on the scale below zero. Every year, more than 60% of students in the United States receive a Lexile measure via reading assessments that report Lexile measures. With dozens of reading programs and assessments reporting out Lexile measures for students, it is a universal scale; just as many different temperature gauges report out Fahrenheit temperatures, many different reading assessments report out Lexile measures.

The Lexile Framework for Reading allows us to:

- Compare students based on national norms (a 50th percentile second-grade student is at 355L; a 75th percentile fifth-grade student is at 1,075L).

- Track growth for students to ensure that they are growing at the appropriate pace (typical third-grade students grow at 113L per year; a typical sixth-grade student grows at 76L per year).

- Match students to texts and books of appropriate complexity, so that they can read material that they find challenging, but not frustrating.

Hopefully, this conveys the benefits of having a standardized, universal measurement scale for both student ability and text complexity. But now let's take the conversation back to listening. In 2018 and 2019, Listenwise teamed up with MetaMetrics (the makers of the Lexile reading scale) to develop the Lexile Framework for Listening. This brings together all the benefits of a reading scale and applies them to listening and, finally, resolves the challenges we described at the beginning of this section.

Now, we can measure a student's skills in reading and listening comprehension on the *same* Lexile scale, so that they can be compared directly. We can also match the student to "just right" audio, too. In Figure 7.7, the student profiled is stronger in listening skills than reading skills, and can be challenged with more complex audio.

Assessing student listening ability is usually accomplished by means of a 30-item test that takes around 30 minutes, where

Figure 7.7 Lexile text measure and Lexile audio measure. *Source:* MetaMetrics.

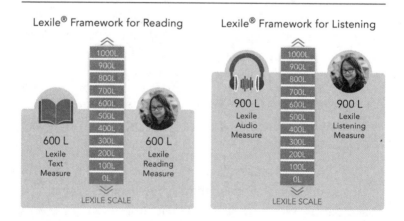

students listen to audio and answer questions. Yes, it takes time and many teachers and parents feel they would rather be using that time for teaching. But, these listening exercises are good for developing students' ability to concentrate and extract meaning from texts, and they provide practice for end-of-year state exams, in those states that assess listening. But the real benefit is that it provides useful information to the teacher that they would not otherwise have.

> *I liked the format of a multiple-choice quiz instead of having to input our answers because it's (1) easier and faster and (2) multiple choice is better because I must know the facts whereas inputting my own answer, it's often possible to waffle through an answer and not understand what the question is asking.*
> —High school history student, California

Take, for example, Benjamin, a fourth-grade student. His Lexile Reading measure is 350L and his Lexile Listening measure is 800L. His listening measure is on-grade, which shows good comprehension skills, but his reading measure is about 450L below where we would expect it to be. His teacher may want to investigate further to check whether he has a reading disability. His comprehending is good, which implies his vocabulary knowledge is also strong, but he may have problems with decoding words on the page. His teacher should consider giving him more listening practice, especially in relevant content areas, to strengthen his overall comprehension, since building vocabulary and background knowledge improves reading comprehension.

Or take Sally, a third-grade student. Her Lexile Reading measure is 250L and her Lexile Listening measure is 280L. Both measures are more typical of a first-grade student at this time of year. Her teacher already knew she struggled with reading but never knew that she struggled with listening, too! Now her teacher knows that Sally may not understand verbal instructions that well and must tailor teaching strategies accordingly. This really necessitates checking that Sally understands class presentations and instructions to develop her listening comprehension skills.

So far so good, but how about measuring the complexity of audio in order to match students with resources at an appropriate level? Listenwise provides podcasts, which range from easy-to-understand to much more complex, so how are these placed on the scale? If you recall, the Lexile Framework for Reading uses a computer algorithm to analyze texts for features like sentence complexity, vocabulary sophistication, and amount of information within and across sentences. But until recently, nothing like this scale existed for audio.

It was impossible for teachers to know if a podcast had densely complex sentences with a high level of vocabulary or was a conversational discussion that was easy to understand. Teachers don't have time to listen and review every piece of audio before assigning it to students. This has been a huge impediment to using audio in the classroom.

The new Lexile Framework for Listening overcomes these barriers. It is also a computer algorithm that does very much the same thing as the reading measure, except that it is tuned to analyze audio files. It analyzes both the *words* and *content* of what the speaker says, which are shown on the left hand side of Figure 7.8, as well as the speaker's *delivery* and *how they say it*, which is shown on the right hand side of the figure.

The research leading to the development of the Lexile Framework for Listening yielded three surprising results.

First, as you would expect, speech that contains meandering sentences, a high density of new information, and sophisticated vocabulary, make audio passages more difficult. This is to be expected; the same characteristics make reading passages difficult, too.

In terms of acoustic features, we saw some unexpected patterns. We imagined that speech rate (i.e., how fast you speak)

Figure 7.8 The four quadrants of audio analysis.
Source: MetaMetrics.

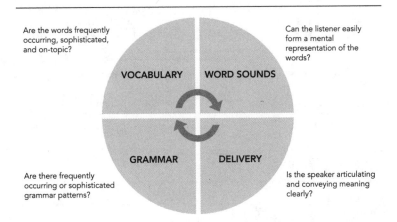

Are the words frequently occurring, sophisticated, and on-topic?

Can the listener easily form a mental representation of the words?

VOCABULARY   WORD SOUNDS

GRAMMAR   DELIVERY

Are there frequently occurring or sophisticated grammar patterns?

Is the speaker articulating and conveying meaning clearly?

would contribute to audio complexity. But as it turns out, faster speech does *not* make audio more difficult to comprehend. However, the length and frequency of *pausing* does contribute to complexity. That is, if the speaker pauses a lot at phrase boundaries, pauses between sentences, or gives long pauses between new pieces of information, then the audio passage is much easier for the student to understand. If you want people to understand your message more easily, don't speak slower; instead, put in some strategic pauses. Understanding speech involves real-time, rapid mental processing, and pauses do two useful things: they chunk the information into bite-sized pieces for the listener; and they assist the listener with processing one piece of information before the next piece is presented. The right pause at the right time really makes a difference for comprehension.

Other acoustic features related to audio complexity include: How clearly are words articulated? How much intonation is used? And, how many words are used that sound similar to other words, for example, time and thyme? All of these can facilitate or impair mental processing of the speech stream. See Figure 7.9 to further understand what features can make audio easy or

Figure 7.9 Audio features that impact level of difficulty.
Source: MetaMetrics.

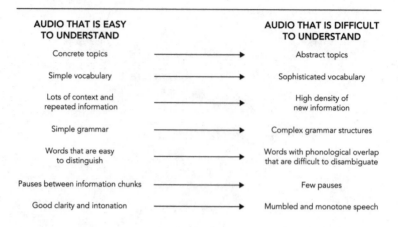

AUDIO THAT IS EASY TO UNDERSTAND		AUDIO THAT IS DIFFICULT TO UNDERSTAND
Concrete topics	⟶	Abstract topics
Simple vocabulary	⟶	Sophisticated vocabulary
Lots of context and repeated information	⟶	High density of new information
Simple grammar	⟶	Complex grammar structures
Words that are easy to distinguish	⟶	Words with phonological overlap that are difficult to disambiguate
Pauses between information chunks	⟶	Few pauses
Good clarity and intonation	⟶	Mumbled and monotone speech

difficult to understand. So, if you want to produce audio that is easier to understand, put in plenty of pauses, vary your intonation to convey your message, and articulate clearly—these are guidelines that newsreaders have always known, but now there is an empirical, scientific model that has weighted all these factors.

Second, we have now quantified the correlation between reading and listening ability in K–12 students, which, statistically speaking, is $r = 0.77$, which is relatively high. If you are familiar with statistics, this will mean something to you, but if you aren't, it means that, generally speaking, better readers are better listeners and vice versa. But, this is not the case for *all* students, and some do *not* fit this pattern. Some students improve in one skill but have a deficit in the other skill. Again, we have always known this due to other research, but now it is quantified.

In reading, it is known that the strongest second-grade students read about as well as the weakest 10th-grade students. We now also have evidence that the very same is true for listening skills! This is a big finding: students do *not* get better at listening as they get older, just by listening more. Rather, the skill of listening, which involves deciphering meaning and processing information, is an academic skill that needs to be developed. It goes well beyond having ears. Once information has been received, whether it is via the medium of print or audio, comprehension requires that deliberate cognitive strategies are activated in order to make meaning.

> **Key Finding:** Students do *not* get better at listening as they get older, just by listening more. Rather, the skill of listening, which involves deciphering meaning and processing information, is an academic skill that needs to be developed.

Third, research on the listening scale revealed another surprising fact about the relationship between reading and listening and how it changes as students progress through the grade levels. It has previously been asserted that:

"Students listen two or three grade levels above their reading."

But the Lexile research has a new finding, that goes like this:

"Yes, students typically listen two or three grade levels above their reading in the lower elementary grades.

"By middle school, students are equally proficient at processing information, whether it is in print or audio.

"By high school, proficient readers actually prefer to process complex information via print than listening. They read better than they listen."

Let's think about this. A typical seven-year-old is still learning to decode printed words. They find it difficult to make meaning from text because they have to spend so much of their cognitive resources figuring out how to sound out all the words. On the other hand, they have been listening to everything that goes on around them since they were born. So they are quite capable of listening to their caregiver or teacher (when they feel like it). If the *same information* is presented to a seven-year-old in print and in audio, they would typically process it better as audio. In addition, most printed texts aimed at younger students contain language and information that is familiar through oral language.

In contrast, a typical 17-year-old who is getting ready for college has done a whole lot of reading to learn complex subject matter. When they are reading, they can linger on difficult sentences, reread and think about it, infer meaning, integrate new knowledge with existing knowledge, and then continue at their own pace. But, when they are listening to complex information, the words pass by them rapidly, and they have to form a mental representation of words while processing meaning. Pausing and replaying an audio file can make it easier, but there is still a lot of parsing that must be done if the information is dense and if words or concepts are unfamiliar. For these students, when complex or technical information is presented to them, it is usually easier to digest in print form. And academic texts aimed at older readers often include new and unfamiliar vocabulary and concepts, which require more attention and metacognitive strategies to comprehend. So, in some respects, reading skills actually "overtake" listening skills, at least for skilled readers.

THE FUTURE OF LISTENING

It's vital that we improve our listening skills. Why? Because we will be doing much more listening very soon in our everyday lives.

"There is a change coming," Julian Treasure, an expert on listening and communication, told me in an interview. The change will be driven by artificial intelligence or AI.

"We will be relating to the internet largely through speech and listening in very short order. We already have Alexa, Siri, and so on. Now, they're going to become much, much, much more intelligent over the next few years." Treasure predicts in the next 5–10 years our interface with the internet will be primarily through speaking and listening.

Already more than 30% of U.S. households have a smart speaker with a personal assistant.[2] And all smartphones are voice-enabled. Forecasts suggest that by 2024, the number of digital voice assistants will reach 8.4 billion units—a number higher than the world's population.[3] To use a digital voice assistant, you must be listening.

A 2019 study found that asking smart speakers or smartphones for information instead of typing your query into a browser hasn't taken over . . . yet. But each year the survey is conducted, more people are asking their smartphones or speakers questions rather than typing them into Google. And they are listening to the replies more frequently. Voice interfaces are happening quickly in the areas of health care, business, and banking. Companies are starting to think about how touchpoints on a website are transforming to listening points. Education is trying to keep up.

In July 2019, Amazon Web Services and SXSW EDU, a major education innovation conference, issued a challenge to edtech companies to design an Alexa-based tool that would transform education. The judge's choice was SayKid, the first screenless, play-based learning platform. They create educational games on Alexa and deliver them through a soft robot. No screen time or typing. It is all voice enabled.

The future of teaching and learning will certainly be altered by AI voice-enabled internet devices. It's possible more curriculum will be delivered over voice-enabled speakers. Learners could listen to lectures, podcasts, or presentations. They could speak their answers and have them automatically transcribed and submitted with a voice command. An AI-enabled listening device could understand a right answer from a wrong answer and correct a student in real time. These future possibilities all hinge on better listening comprehension skills.

Thank you to Alistair Van Moere, Chief Product Officer at MetaMetrics, for his invaluable contributions to this chapter.

References

1. Hogan, T.P., Adlof, S.M., & Alonzo, C. (2014). On the importance of listening comprehension. *International Journal of Speech-Language Pathology*, 16(3), 199–207. doi: 10.3109/17549507.2014.904441.

2. Statista Research Department. (2020, August 27). Smart speaker U.S. household ownership 2019. Statista, https://www.statista.com/statistics/791575/us-smart-speaker-household-ownership/ (accessed October 1, 2020).

3. Statista Research Department. (2020, September 23). Number of voice assistants in use worldwide 2019–2024. Statista, https://www.statista.com/statistics/973815/worldwide-digital-voice-assistant-in-use/ (accessed October 1, 2020).

Chapter 8

Creating Podcasts

On the way to school, Vicki has a 30-minute commute. It's not too bad at 6:30 in the morning. For the first part of her commute, Vicki is thinking about the day ahead and is going over her lesson plans in her head. But after she feels confident and ready for the day, she wants a distraction.

That's when she puts on an episode of her favorite podcast. Right now, it's "Dolly Parton's America." The podcast is about Dolly's career and influence in America. But it touches on politics, feminism, class, and race, through the experiences of one of the most famous country singers.

After the first two minutes Vicki is hooked, deep into the story. Her drive flies by and she is sitting in the school parking lot thinking that if her students could tell a compelling story like the host and producers do in this podcast, they could learn so much. They could make it a personal narrative. Or by interviewing others, they could learn how their lives, like Dolly's, intersect with the currents of society and are shaped by race and class.

The Dolly Parton podcast is fact-based, draws on multiple sources, flows with a coherent storyline, and successfully communicates information. Isn't that what all students should demonstrate in their learning?

The light bulb goes off. Maybe her students should make a podcast, Vicki thinks.

PODCASTING IN EDUCATION

The first audio storytelling show I remember listening to was Paul Harvey's "The Rest of the Story." In middle and high school, we carpooled with the neighbors who lived down the street. Every morning my friend's mother crammed four kids in her Toyota Corona and turned up ABC News. I don't remember what time we drove to school every morning, but it was always during Paul Harvey's segment called "The Rest of the Story." His stories were short, less than four minutes long, and uncovered an interesting fact about a famous person or historic event. They were a master class in storytelling. You never knew until the very end who or what he was talking about. I wanted to write stories like Paul Harvey. If my teachers had given me an audio writing assignment, I would have been thrilled.

Students who are listening to mentor podcasts are learning what good writing sounds like. They can use their listening skills to be active learners, listen to others, and create their own podcasts. Writing a podcast helps students develop foundational literacy skills. Because students can podcast about any subject, they will be learning to read, write, speak, and listen in a variety of content areas. Podcasting, especially when done in small groups, fosters creativity, communication, collaboration, and critical thinking, among other 21st-century skills outlined by the Framework for 21st Century Learning.[1]

It promotes social-emotional learning as defined by CASEL, the Collaborative for Academic, Social and Emotional Learning. CASEL has a framework for addressing social and emotional learning (SEL). Creating podcasts with other people touches on the important SEL goals of understanding emotions (listening for how people say things, i.e., prosody), showing empathy for others (listening to and recording others), establishing positive relationships (working together in groups to create a podcast), and making responsible decisions in the editing, writing, and review process (collaborating on a podcast).

Students are drawn to expressing themselves through podcasting. Not only can they emulate real journalists and famous podcasters, learning about writer's craft, but they are deeply engaged in their learning when they are producing something meaningful for an audience. Personalized learning has become a buzzword in education. And there's debate about what "personalized learning" really means. But it's fair to say that when students create their own podcasts, they are empowered with agency to make choices, which makes them active participants in their learning. They are engaged in designing their own learning experiences by actively exploring real-world issues and problems, developing ideas and theories, and pursuing answers and solutions. According to research by the Hanover Research Group, "autonomy is generally associated with greater personal well-being and satisfaction in educational environments, as well as in terms of academic performance."[2]

> *When kids are creating anything, they are learning implicitly as well as whatever explicit content you are wanting them to learn. But in the case of a podcast . . . it puts kids in the position of having to teach someone something or at least share information with an audience. When kids are asked to learn something that will be used to teach someone else that thing, they just learn it a lot better.*
>
> —Katie Rogers, eighth-grade Math/Algebra 1 teacher, Brooklyn, NY

Recording and sharing their learning validates their voices and their knowledge in a way that is motivating and empowering.[3] Podcasting provides alternative modalities through which students can demonstrate their learning and meet curriculum standards. Writing podcasts help students reconsider and modify their ideas during content creation.[4] If you are tired of the stand and deliver presentations, or Prezi or PowerPoint, so are your students.

Not all students want the stress of standing in front of the class and presenting live. Some students are the type of learner who wants to plan out and script something after extensive research, versus "on the spot" public speaking. Podcasts help students reflect on their learning through listening to their own oral performance.[5]

It can also give your students an audience beyond the school walls. They are creating something that will have an authentic audience, which motivates them to do their best work.

THE PODCAST EXPLOSION

In the past 10 years, there's been a sea change in the way we consume audio. Terrestrial radio broadcast stations, both AM and FM, are losing listeners as more people listen to HD radio, satellite radio, and, of course, audio over the internet. More than any other time in history, people are creating audio, wanting to be heard. They are connecting with like-minded people who they otherwise wouldn't be able to reach. There has been an explosion in podcasts and a resurgence in people listening to audio.

Audio has become so portable and easy to access, with a wide variety of content that people are listening while driving, exercising, cooking, gardening, walking, flying, and the list goes on.

The word "podcast" was created by a journalist looking for a new term to describe the mash up between iPods and broadcast media. The Merriam-Webster dictionary defines a podcast as a program, either music or talking, that's made available in digital format for automatic download over the internet.

As of January 2021, there were more than 1.75 million podcasts with more than 43 million episodes.[6] According to the Spoken Word Audio Report, spoken word listening has increased 30% in the last six years.[7] And the growth is driven by large increases among women, younger listeners, African Americans, and Latinos. Three quarters of all Americans listen to spoken word audio each month; 43% listen daily. The age category with the largest increase in listening is 13- to 34-year-olds. These podcast fans may include some of your students. Ask them what their favorite podcasts are.

The podcast medium has quickly become a crowded space with big players making millions of dollars hosting compelling podcasts. That has created an arms race for excellent podcast content. In 2020, Spotify paid $100 million to make "The Joe Rogan Experience" show exclusive to Spotify.[8] It's one of podcasting's longest-running and most popular shows. I share a list of good podcasts in Chapter 2; below are some other favorites I suggest you check out.

Monica's Favorite Podcasts
- *Embedded*—The host takes you deep behind a news story with several episodes about a topic. I enjoyed the Essential Mitch season.
- *Slow Burn*—A podcast that dissects some of the biggest news stories of the century. I loved the Clinton impeachment season.
- *Planet Money*—I don't understand economics well, but this podcast makes me think I do.
- *Rough Translation*—Because I lived abroad, I love hearing the quirky, yet relevant stories in this podcast.
- *Hurry Slowly*—A podcast about finding calm by slowing down, something I should do more often, but at least I can listen to a podcast about it.

- *How I Built This*—As an entrepreneur, hearing the stories of other founders is inspiring.

Podcasts Students Will Enjoy In or Out of Class

- **Elementary School**

  o *Story Pirates*—The creators take kids' story ideas and turn them into funny comedy sketches. A real audio drama.

  o *Tumble*—A science podcast for kids that's also interesting for adults because it explores cool scientific questions like what's at the center of the earth.

  o *Short and Curley*—An ethics podcast for kids might sound strange, but kids like thinking about sticky questions such as Do the ends justify the means? Plus, it's super well produced with music and sound effects.

  o *Good Sport*—Professional athletes share their stories about when they were kids, making kids feel like they can do anything!

- **Middle School**

  o *The Unexplainable Disappearance of Mars Patel*—A Peabody-winning serial mystery podcast about a middle school kid, performed by middle school kids.

  o *Brains On!*—A science podcast for kids and curious adults exploring some hard science questions and behavioral questions such as why is it so hard to break a habit?

  o *Smash Boom Best*—A debate show that pits ants against bees, ice cream against French fries, and lets the listeners debate and decide which is best.

  o *The Book Club for Kids*—Learn about a new book from the students who read it and hear them interview the author who wrote it.

  o *Welcome to Night Vale*—A fictitious town's fictitious news makes for a creepy podcast.

- **High School**
  - o *Radiolab*—I always learn something fascinating from this podcast because it challenges your preconceived notions about how the world works. There is now a Radiolab for kids that's appropriate for middle school and younger students.
  - o *This American Life*—The podcast picks a theme and shares several stories around the theme in "acts" during each episode. Some of the subjects might be inappropriate for teenagers.
  - o *Wait Wait . . . Don't Tell Me!*—A weekly news quiz show that will make kids laugh and learn something.
  - o *TED Radio Hour*—The host explores a big idea through TED talk snippets and interviews with some of world's biggest thinkers.

PODCAST CREATION DEEPENS LEARNING

You have the ability to help your students create their own podcasts to deepen their learning, develop agency, and present what they know in their own voices. Podcasting by students represents a fundamental tenet of learning—students must master a subject in order to teach others about it. That transference of knowledge is one of the most powerful tools of education. And with podcasting, it's fun and easy to do.

> By creating a podcast, my students learned about public speaking skills and how your voice really matters and how you say things matter. They learned how to tell their story to a global audience.
> —Rayna Freedman, fifth-grade teacher,
> Mansfield, MA

How would you like to assign one project that helps students practice their reading and writing skills, builds knowledge in a subject they care about, lets them be creative and authentic, and is fun to do alone or in groups? Student podcasting is a great way to address all of those goals. Even for elementary teachers, recording and sharing students' voices builds important skills. And yet many teachers are so intimidated by the technology and the steps involved in producing a podcasting project, they convince themselves they can't do it. I will get to the technology part of making podcasts, but right now let's talk about the amazing educational benefits.

In our work at Listenwise advising and training teachers to make podcasts with their students, we've seen how it develops literacy skills, builds and reinforces content knowledge, fosters creativity, personalizes learning, and offers authentic audiences for students' work. It also provides students with alternate modalities through which to showcase their learning.

Student-produced podcasts can empower students to become more active and independent learners.[9] A 2007 study examining the educational value of student-produced podcasts asked medical students to make podcasts about an ethical issue surrounding genetics in order to educate other medical students. Thirty students were divided into five groups. The group project lasted about three weeks and they created podcasts between 5 and 10 minutes long.

The study found many benefits including students reporting that making podcasts made them more motivated to learn, helped their cognitive learning, and taught them how to work well together in groups. These are all highly valuable, transferable skills.

Another study at the university level found that student-created podcasts improved their understanding of topics covered in lectures because they revisited the content as they created the podcast.[10] It also improved the way they interacted with their professors and they reported that it was a fun and interactive activity to do with their peers. The research found "the podcasts enable students to develop independent learning skills," while at the same time connect them with their peers. Podcasting also offers a new way to assess student learning.

Podcasting in Remote Learning

Whether your students are physically in a classroom working together or collaborating remotely, podcasting can bring them together. In education, the COVID-19 epidemic caused a seismic shift to remote learning. It isolated teachers from their students and students from their peers. Until the temporary closures of almost all schools, distance learning was experienced by only a fraction of the K–12 student population. Today, every teacher, in every school, at every grade level, must be prepared to teach in a fully remote digital environment.

Enabling your students to create podcasts can help connect them to each other and to people and events beyond the walls of their homes or their classrooms. As you'll learn later, we recommend that students create podcasts in groups. This fosters collaboration. Students learn from each other's questions and research. They can share their opinions in a safe space and learn from different perspectives. This can be done online. Listenwise has a free podcasting toolkit that offers step-by-step instructions for podcasting with students in classrooms or remotely that can be found at https://listenwise.com/book.

One study on the challenges of distance learning at the university level evaluated the potential of podcasting to enhance remote learning. The study found student-created podcasts promoted a sense of belonging to a learning community and reduced students' feelings of isolation and anxiety. It found that podcasts created by professors and tutors to reinforce concepts taught in online classes had a positive impact on the learning community. It also found that the podcasts "counteracted the negative implications that result from students' physical separation."[11]

Although this chapter is devoted mostly to how you can help your students create podcasts, you might reflect on how you could also create audio of your own to connect with your students when teaching remotely.

Class Activity: Steal the Form

High School Students: One of the most popular podcasts that propelled the genre forward is *Serial*, which launched in 2014. The podcast, which was made for an adult audience, centers on the crime of a murdered teenage Korean American girl by her ex-boyfriend who is Pakistani American. Or at least that's what the criminal justice system decided. The ex-boyfriend is in jail and the host, Sarah Koenig, is reviewing the case in detail. She is as much a character in the story, with the open-ended questions she poses to the listener and her shared confusion, as the people she interviews to see if she believes the ex-boyfriend is really guilty. Many high school teachers use the podcast to teach literary nonfiction and cover the Common Core ELA standards in reading, writing, speaking, and listening. They use it to teach problem-solving skills using primary sources as well as author choice and bias, and direct and indirect characterization.

Michael Godsey, formerly a 10th-grade English teacher and now a school administrator, was an early adopter of teaching with podcasts and authored many of those lessons. He uses podcasts to develop critical thinking and authentic engagement among his students. Godsey says using *Serial* was a huge academic success because students were engaged in critical thinking, listening comprehension, and the art of storytelling. Michael's full lessons on *Serial* can be found on TeachersPay Teachers.com, an online marketplace for lesson plans. TeachersPayTeachers reported that their annual downloads of lessons based on podcasts increased 650% in 2014.[12]

In addition to creating lessons on the *Serial* podcast, Godsey also created a set of lessons to help ELA teachers guide students to create their own podcasts by critically listening and imitating other podcasts. The following is an excerpt of one of his lessons.

Technical Notes
Time: About two hours

Background
This exercise is a step in the scaffolding process toward students writing their own podcasts. Students identify the story elements before modeling their own stories after it.

Basic Sequence of Lesson
1. Choose a podcast episode that you'd like to use as a model for your students, preferably one with transcripts. We recommend "Is This Working?" from *This American Life*. Or you could choose another podcast of interest on Listenwise.
2. Recreate and distribute the worksheet shown on the following page.
3. We highly recommend making copies of the transcript (or projecting it on a screen) for your students so that they can read along as they listen.
4. Play the episode and pause at the end of each part of the story.
5. At each pause, ask students to label the story element and summarize it on their worksheets. You may allow them to describe the story element in place of a label (e.g., "It gets the listeners' attention" may replace "hook").
6. When the episode (and the corresponding analysis) is complete, ask the students to create their own outline of a similar story/podcast, using the story elements on the worksheet as a guide. We recommend doing this in groups, but students can do this individually if you prefer. Students should not write an entire script—that would take too long for this exercise. It's enough that they have a general idea for their story.
7. Finally, ask them to compare and contrast their stories with the featured podcast. Answers could include length of time, degree of importance to the overall text, and/or which one was superior (and why).
8. Option: Instead of listening to the entire episode before they write their own outline, you can break it up by listening to one part (or a few parts) of the podcast at a time. For example, you could play the introduction, have the students invent their own introduction, and then go back to listening to the next part.

Instructions

Worksheet: For each story element, summarize your model's version, summarize your version, and then explain how they compare. For example, you might summarize the introduction of the podcast you listened to, then summarize your introduction, and then compare the two ("Just like the other podcast, we tried to hook the listeners' attention with a provocative question followed by some scientific theories; ours was shorter and funnier, but not as detailed").

1. Story Element:
   Podcast's version: _____
   Your group's version: _____
   How they compare: _____
   (Create a handout with at least 8 of these story elements to distribute.)
   (Source: Michael Godsey, Podcasts in the Classroom)

Podcasting fosters collaboration beyond the school walls. Let me give you an example. Dan Kearney's eighth-grade history class from Orange County, California did a podcast series on immigration called *History Lessons in Immigration*. One student, a 13-year-old, created her podcast to learn more about her family's immigration story by interviewing her relatives. She starts the podcast by saying that "she thought she knew the story of her grandmothers' emigration to America," but as it turns out she had a lot to learn. To learn how her grandmother came from the Philippines to America, she interviewed her dad, her uncle, and her grandmother, who was 76 years old and lived in another city. The interviews were on the phone, online, and in person. From the audio she pieced together her family's immigration story.

The student also learned about important parts of world history through her grandmother's experience. In 1942, her grandfather was forced into the Bataan Death March after the Japanese invaded the Philippines. As part of her family history narrative, she explains what the death march was to her listeners, which was an excellent learning experience for her.

At the end, she reflects on how meaningful it was speaking with her relatives to learn the true story of her family's past.

> **Listening to Student Work**
>
> You can listen to student work on the podcast I created and host called *The Student Podcast Podcast*.[13] In each episode, you'll hear excerpts of students' work and interviews with the teachers who made it happen. Here are some episodes I recommend:
>
> **Third-grade podcast:** "A Service-Learning Podcasting Project": Students visit a food pantry to learn more about hunger in the community.
>
> **Fifth-grade podcast:** "Debunking Myths and Stereotypes through Podcasting": Students use their voices to debunk myths about modern life on Native American reservations.
>
> **High school:** "Podcasting with Clubs": In an afterschool club, students create a podcast that examines the concept of academic identity.

Making Podcasts

When my oldest daughter was in kindergarten, I was working as a reporter at WBUR, Boston's NPR station. I became friendly with her teacher and would often get permission to bring in my recorder to capture a song at circle time or special projects. The teacher asked if I could help make a podcast with the students and their parents exploring their memories. The unit brought together the students and one of their parents or caregivers to talk about their favorite childhood memory. The question was simple, "What's your favorite childhood memory?" Each child asked their parent for a memory and then the parent asked their children, who were five years old at the time, the same question.

In this case, I was the audio recorder and editor. I sat in on every interview, which took place in the storage closet because it was quiet. The stories were joyful and fun for the kids to learn something about their parents at their age. And, of course, the kids loved sharing their own stories. One I remember well was a father telling the story of when he was eight years old and took a train with his dad from Connecticut to Detroit to buy a new car. He remembered how in the 1970s, when Detroit was a 24-hour city making cars day and night, he was amazed that the city was alive all night and that they ate at an all-night diner. His daughter remembered going to an amusement park and riding the rollercoaster.

Allowing students to be heard by their parents and by their peers is powerful.

As the project with kindergarteners demonstrates, there is no minimum age for students to create podcasts. You just need to be more of a participant in the recording and editing with younger podcasters.

Five Steps to Begin a Podcasting Project

1. Listen to Podcasts as Mentor Texts

In order to set high expectations for your classroom podcasting projects, begin by engaging your students in listening to high-quality podcasts. These podcasts can serve as mentor audio stories, just as you would use a mentor text to demonstrate excellent writing style. These audio stories should be deconstructed just as any other text. They should be examined for the way they are written, the words the podcasters use, the structures of the sentences, and the narrative arcs of the stories.

2. Set a Purpose

After sharing great audio stories with students, you should select a purpose for the student-created podcasts that aligns with your curriculum. You begin by selecting one of three general purposes for a podcast:

Inform, persuade, or entertain.

Is the purpose to research specific curriculum topics so they engage in deeper thinking and do their own investigating?

Is the project focused on students telling their own stories? Or reflecting on something they are learning?

Do you want your students to develop awareness and understanding of world events? Or focus on local community issues? Or an issue at the school?

Should students be focusing on making arguments for a particular viewpoint or policy or persuading people to act through a PSA?

3. Select a Genre

Students can create podcasts of many different genres. You are probably familiar with the genres of popular podcasts. They include comedy, news, sports, society and culture, and true crime, to name a few. You might start by discussing these podcast genres with your students, as they likely have their favorites.

In the K–12 context, the genre of podcasts you'll be creating may be more aligned to typical composition genres. Think about what kind of writing you might ask students to do and then consider having students create a podcast instead of a paper.

You should also think about which genre best suits your curriculum goals. Do you want your students to express their opinions? Debate others? Consider multiple perspectives? Compile factual reports?

Consider, for example, taking the personal narrative topic in your curriculum and turning it into a podcast project. Or doing a book review as a podcast. If you are teaching persuasive writing, students could create public service announcements, or PSA podcasts. If they are learning about argument, they could create a podcast in which they interview people with different viewpoints. Students going on a field trip could interview people on site. The possibilities are endless.

Suggestions for podcasting with students of different ages.

Elementary School Students: Creating podcasts with younger students will be more teacher led. It's best to select a simple, personal topic. Ask for a memory or an opinion. Keep the question prompts short and clear. Don't group your students, record them individually. At this age, students can't be expected to operate the recording and editing tools. You need to be the recorder and editor. Each podcast or interview should be less than two minutes and only cover one topic.

> *I think the doing is far more important than what you end up producing in the end.*
> —David Green, third-grade teacher,
> Winnetka, IL

Middle School Students: Select a topic related to your curriculum. Students will be able to operate the recording and editing software, so they can be put into groups. If they are going to interview people outside the classroom, keep the questions short and only do one interview. At this age, students like to interview each other and share their opinions about a book, a news topic, or a topic of interest. They might be less comfortable sharing personal topics.

> *Kids are natural storytellers.*
> —Matt Stokes, eighth-grade Math/Algebra
> 1 teacher, Brooklyn, NY

High School Students: Select a topic that's highly relevant to your students. Ask them what they want to explore about their world, their studies, their future, or themselves. At this age,

students are more likely to be comfortable with self-explora-
tion. They can be expected to operate all the technology on
their own. Working in groups or individually, students will be
able to interview people outside their classroom.

> *Making a podcast was one of the favorite things*
> *I did in class as a teacher.*
> —Michael Godsey, former high school ELA
> teacher, Paso Robles, CA

4. Choose a Production Format

In addition to thinking about what you are producing, you need
to think about how you are producing it. It is important to define
the production format of student podcasts at the outset based on
your level of experience. Obviously, there are many different formats, but for simplicity's sake, we have distilled it down to three
production formats that work well with student podcasting in the
K–12 setting. They include single voice, conversation, and report.

Formats (in order of degree of production difficulty)

1. Single voice

2. Conversation

3. Report

> You can download a Podcasting Toolkit with
> more detailed instructions at https://listen
> wise.com/book.

Single Voice—The most basic format for podcasts involves
one voice reading a script. Students could be reflecting on a
topic they have learned about, narrating an experience, sharing commentary about an issue, or reviewing a book or movie.
This format can include music or sound effects, but it includes
only one person speaking.

Conversation—This podcast format typically includes two or three voices in a conversation about an event, topic, or issue. Students will need to write a script for the conversation that may be followed word-for-word or used as a general guide.

Report—This podcast format is more complex and is similar to what you would hear on NPR. A report has a well-scripted narration and includes interviews of several people either inside or outside the classroom, music or sound effects, and substantive editing.

Teacher Podcast Lesson Example

Let me give you an example of a podcast using the Single Voice format and the Commentary genre. It may surprise you. You are probably familiar with the format. It's one person's perspective in a straightforward way. Often it uses facts to back up opinions.

Ninth grade World History teacher Sarah Pesaturo from Newton, Massachusetts, had her students create a five-minute commentary in which they made an evidence-based argument for the historical question, "Do the Boxers deserve a bad reputation?" The "Boxers" were what foreigners called a Chinese secret society that led an uprising from 1899-1901 in northern China against the spread of Western and Japanese influence. This all sounds pretty boring to a ninth grader, right? But you should hear their podcasts!

Sarah's students were graded on how well they cited textual evidence to support their argument (a language arts standard). She said it was "awesome" to teach through the lens of podcasting because students understood why they would need evidence to back up their points. They also had to practice summarizing/synthesis skills for writing (also a language arts standard) because their podcasts had to be a certain length. They had to figure out what was the most important information to include within the designated time frame.

Sarah said her students also practiced writing an informative text as a podcast script, which was a great way to get them used to the writing process without having the daunting task of creating a typical five-page research paper. And she liked that they were able to practice oral skills that are not usually assessed in the classroom. And they got to do it in a private environment, which took the pressure off from speaking to the entire class.

5. Group Students

Podcasting might sound like it is a solo activity. It is not. Behind every great voice you hear is a production staff that includes writers, researchers, producers, audio engineers, and editors. It's a collaboration, and it should be a collaborative project with your students.

Research shows how working together on a product that students know will be shared with others has multiple benefits. First, it fosters development of important collaboration skills. Each person in the group must contribute in some way, and the others must listen and absorb their contribution. In one study, students found that developing podcasts together was a "valuable way to enhance team-working skills."[14] They were able to identify their key strengths and use them to contribute to the podcasts by selecting the roles they would play in the production. They had to plan together as a team, share responsibility, and allocate tasks. They had to make sure each member made an equal contribution to the project. The project required them to plan in advance and have clear roles and expectations. If one person faltered in their role, the whole podcast was in jeopardy.

Many teachers have told me they've been pleasantly surprised by how students who are often silent in class become super involved in podcasting projects. It's a good idea to allow students to self-select their roles. There is built-in natural accountability, as a successful podcast requires that everyone do their part.

Standards

As demonstrated in the example of Sarah's ninth-grade class writing a commentary about the Boxer Rebellion, podcasting projects address multiple curriculum standards. Students are demonstrating their knowledge of a subject, writing, synthesizing information, and much more.

> *I feel like my students learned so many things, so many skills. Of course, the 4 Cs in education. Collaboration. They were working together in groups to create this final product. Communication. It was all about the discussions they were having. Critical thinking. One of the focuses of this assignment was to make connections to other things. Creativity. They worked on their writing skills because they drafted the scripts for their podcasts from scratch. Summarizing because they were deciding what to include in these podcasts.*
> —Laura Isenhour, 10th-grade English II World Literature teacher, Hillsborough, NC

In general, the skills involved in a podcasting project include researching, reviewing, writing, drafting, editing, and performing. I want to spend a moment on the repetition of material that's a built-in part of making a podcast. When I was a reporter, I was often assigned a completely new story to cover, which I sometimes had little knowledge about. My first step was always research. The reading I did to familiarize myself with a subject led to me creating a list of people I wanted to interview for the story. I used these interviews to build my background knowledge or potentially for inclusion in my audio report. This step in the reporting process could take days. I undertook my research as I would a thesis paper, knowing that my work would be public to millions of people, many of whom knew the subject better than me.

Researching helped me create a long list of questions for the people I would interview. These recorded interviews, many of them in person to gather the best sound quality, would be 20 minutes to an hour long. The interview was another deeper level of research—primary research. These conversations often led to insights or new information I had not learned in my reading. And, of course, they were recordings that added voice, emotion, and context to the written research. They were the gems of the reporting.

The next step in the reporting process was to transcribe every word from the interviews. I typically took handwritten notes in a reporter's notebook during the conversations and marked the time code of important sentences. Even these written notes were not good enough to serve as a complete reflection of the conversation. I still typed up a written transcript. Most journalists follow this procedure because you want an accurate account of the conversation and you want to solidify your understanding of the subject.

Before the advent of the low to no-cost speech-to-text transcription tools, I did all of this transcription by listening to the recording and typing it out verbatim. It took a long time. A 20-minute interview could easily take 45 minutes to accurately transcribe. But I can assure you, by the end of the transcription process, I knew the content of the interview extremely well.

When it was time to write the script, it came easily. I had already built a narrative in my mind as I was working on the research and interviews. The repetition built into the process of creating a podcast put me in a position of subject mastery as I launched into my creation process.

The same will be true with your students. The skills of researching, reviewing, writing, drafting, and editing all provide multiple opportunities to reinforce the content.

RECORDING AND EDITING TOOLS

There are many free and fee-based audio editing tools that are easy to use in school. All of these tools are digital, and thus, not destructive. What I mean by that is that your students cannot irreparably destroy an audio recording. They could mistakenly delete the whole file, but when they are editing it, they can always undo or restore the edits they've made.

Free Recording Tools

All smartphone have multiple apps for voice recording that are free. I use VoiceMemos on my iPhone, as well as Voice Recorder. The advancements in smartphone technology make these recordings broadcast-quality. Students can record themselves or each other and share the audio or upload it to the cloud. If they are interviewing people who live far away, students could instruct the interviewee to record themselves using a smartphone app and send the audio to the student or teacher.

There are also many web-based podcast recording platforms, such as Zencastr, that allow you to invite people to be interviewed and then record you and your interviewee on separate tracks.

Free Editing Tools

Audacity

Audacity is open source editing software that can be used on any computer. It requires you to download the audio and store it on the computer's hard drive.

Anchor

Anchor is a free app that's downloadable on smartphones. It's designed to make podcasts by giving you the ability to record, edit, and arrange your audio segments.

Paid Editing Tools

Soundtrap

Soundtrap is a cloud-based audio editing software that can be used on any internet connected device. Soundtrap for Education is a paid subscription model for teachers and schools that has excellent privacy protections and allows for teacher control collaborative tools.

Garage Band

Garage Band is installed on Apple devices, such as iPads and Mac-Books, so technically it isn't a paid app, but you need to have an Apple device to use it. It was not designed for podcasting, but for music recording, so there are some necessary steps you need to take to record a podcast, including modifying some of the settings.

As you think about how your students can apply their listening skills to be active learners, I hope you feel ready to assist them in the next step in building their listening skills, creating a podcast.

The podcasters of the future could be in your classroom. Now that you understand the importance of building listening comprehension skills, put them in the driver's seat of their learning with a podcasting project. It will be the perfect culmination of all they've learned from you about being good listeners.

REFLECTION AND PLANNING

Take this opportunity to write some reflections and plans for action.

Imitation is the best form of flattery. Select a style of podcast you would like your students to imitate. See some suggestions of podcasts for students earlier in the chapter. Listen to the style and have students write a short imitation of the style.

How will the project fit into your curriculum? (e.g., Within which unit will the project fit? What will precede the podcasting project?)

What will be the purpose of the project? What will students create? (e.g., learning reflection, book review, public service announcement)

What will be the format of the podcast? (e.g., commentary, conversation, report)

References

1. Battelle for Kids. Frameworks & resources. www.battelle-forkids.org/networks/p21/frameworks-resources.

2. Hanover Research. (2014). *Impact of student choice and personalized learning.* http://www.gssaweb.org/wp-content/uploads/2015/04/Impact-of-Student-Choice-and-Personalized-Learning-1.pdf (accessed September 30, 2020).

3. Nie, M., Cashmore, A., & Cane, C. (2008). *The educational value of student-generated podcasts* (pp. 15–26, Rep.). Leeds, UK: The Association for Learning Technology.

4. Hargis, J., & Wilson, D. (2005). *Fishing for learning with a podcast net*. www.unf.edu/dept/cirt/tech/podcast/Hargis-PodcastArticle.pdf (accessed December 20, 2020).

5. Huann, T.Y., & Thong, M.K. (2006). *Audioblogging and podcasting in education*. Edublog.net, edublog.net/astinus/mt/files/docs/Literature%20Review%20on%20audioblogging%20and%20podcasting.pdf (accessed December 20, 2020).

6. PodcastHosting.org. (2021, January 1). *2021 global podcast statistics, demographics & habits*. podcasthosting.org/podcast-statistics/.

7. National Public Media, and Edison Research. (2020, October). *The 2020 spoken word audio report*. www.nationalpublicmedia.com/insights/reports/the-spoken-word-audio-report/.

8. Spangler, T. (2020, May 19). Joe Rogan will bring his podcast exclusively to Spotify. Yahoo! Finance, https://finance.yahoo.com/news/joe-rogan-bring-podcast-exclusively-183336548.html (accessed September 19, 2020).

9. Nie, M., Cashmore, A., & Cane, C. (2008). *The educational value of student-generated podcasts* (pp. 15–26, Rep.). Leeds, UK: The Association for Learning Technology.

10. Stoltenkamp, J., et al. (2011). Rolling out podcasting to enhance teaching and learning: A case of the University of the Western Cape. *International Journal of Instructional Technology and Distance Learning*, 8(1): 1–21.

11. Lee, M., & Chan, A. (2007). Reducing the effects of isolation and promoting inclusivity for distance learners through podcasting Turkish online. *The Turkish Online Journal of Distance Education*.

12. Godsey, M. (2016, October 17). Using "Serial" to get students to read more. *The Atlantic*, https://www.theatlantic.com/education/archive/2016/03/the-benefits-of-podcasts-in-class/473925/ (accessed September 19, 2020).

13. Brady-Myerov, M. (2019, January). *Student podcast PODCAST*. Listenwise, studentpodcastpodcast.libsyn.com/.

14. Lee, M., & Chan, A. (2007). Reducing the effects of isolation and promoting inclusivity for distance learners through podcasting Turkish online. *The Turkish Online Journal of Distance Education*.

Index